FIXING THE EU INTEL CRISIS

FIXING THE EU INTEL CRISIS

Intelligence Sharing, Law Enforcement and the Threat of Chemical, Biological, and Nuclear Terrorism

MUSA KHAN JALALZAI

Algora Publishing
New York

Library of Congress Cataloging-in-Publication Data —

Names: Jalalzai, Musa Khan, author.
Title: Fixing the EU intelligence crisis: intelligence sharing, law
    enforcement and the threat of chemical biological and nuclear terrorism /
    Musa Khan Jalalzai.
Description: New York: Algora Publishing, [2016] | Includes bibliographical
    references.
Identifiers: LCCN 2016032034 (print) | LCCN 2016035171 (ebook) | ISBN
    9781628942163 (soft cover: alk. paper) | ISBN 9781628942170 (hard cover:
    alk. paper) | ISBN 9781628942187 (pdf)
Subjects: LCSH: Intelligence service—European Union countries. |
    Terrorism—European Union countries—Prevention. | Law
    enforcement—European Union countries—International cooperation. |
    National security—European Union countries. | Security,
    International—European Union countries.
Classification: LCC JN94.A56 I6235 2016 (print) | LCC JN94.A56 (ebook)
| DDC
    327.124—dc23
LC record available at https://lccn.loc.gov/2016032034

TABLE OF CONTENTS

by Diva Patang Wardak

> *A smart man makes a mistake, learns from it, and never*
> *makes that mistake again. But a wise man finds a smart man and*
> *learns from him how to avoid the mistake altogether.*
> — Roy H. Williams

I am grateful to research scholar and intelligence expert Mr. Musa Khan Jalalzai for asking me to write a foreword for his book. In fact, this book is a critical analysis of intelligence sharing at the law enforcement level, and intelligence surveillance cooperation of PRISM, TEMPORA, UPSTREAM, ECHELON, the NSA and the Five-Eye intelligence alliance with the EU member states. Intelligence is more than the organized collection of targeted information, while information processing can include technical issues such as transcribing and translating intercepted telephone conversations. Analysis is a process of determining what the intelligence information means and how it can be brought within the matrix and parameters of institutional network. Interestingly, this is what author Musa Khan Jalalzai has detailed in this excellent book.

Few people who know their intelligence history can have lived through the early years of the twenty-first century without a disturbing sense of déjà vu. Most of the current intelligence problems within the European Union, whether they relate to predicting surprise attacks, the politicization of intelligence, or questions of ethics and privacy are old conundrums. However, it is hard to escape the feeling that closer attention to obvious lessons from the past would have assisted European Union intelligence sharing in avoiding the recent attacks in Paris and Brussels. Indeed, one of the greatest challenges for intelligence studies is to connect intelligence history and current policy. Policy makers are inclined to talk about new threats and certainly some threats, especially those related to globalization, are innovative. It is not only policy makers but also intelligence agencies themselves who have paid little attention to history and historians.

Intelligence and intelligence services are simultaneously necessary for democracy and a threat to it. Researcher Robert Jervis (2009) argues that without a good intelligence, a country will thrash about blindly or allow threats to grow without taking countermeasures. It is right to say that knowledge is power, and perhaps it is more accurate to say that knowledge is needed if power is to be used well. If knowledge contributes to power, then those who have the knowledge are powerful, which is why a poorly regulated intelligence service can menace leaders and citizens. Power without knowledge is useless at best, dangerous at worst.

Government should know as much as possible about threats and opportunities—and in time to do something about them. It is correct to say that the major intelligence failure since the end of the Cold War was not the attack of 9/11; instead, it was the startling lack of attention given to the rise of irregular warfare including insurgency, ISIS, Taliban, extremism, jihadism and the new terrorism, which in fact resemble groups from previous centuries.

Intelligence as information is different from the kind of everyday information one can find in the local library, because intelligence usually has a secret component. The nation seeks to know much more, though, than warnings about potential attacks, which are not prevented because of the lack of intelligence sharing between 28 states of the European Union. We all knew that an attack would be taking place in Europe and we also know that Britain may be next on the list for a surprise attack.

The intelligence agencies face quite a challenge in meeting the government's needs for insightful information about threats and opportunities. The world has some 191 countries and an untold number of organizations and groups, many of which are hostile toward European countries. These adversaries have become skillful in hiding their plans and operations from the prying eyes of espionage agents and spy machines.

If all European Union intelligence agencies share information accordingly, these adversaries will not be able to hide their plans and operations. Therefore, the principal challenge to EU intelligence now is to collect information that adversaries want to keep secret and share it with other European Union countries to avoid surprises. This is the most important phase of the intelligence cycle, since information that is not collected cannot be used. Collecting strategically relevant information is harder today than in the second half of the Cold War.

Whatever causes intelligence operations to fail, intentionally or accidentally, through action or inaction, is an enemy of intelligence. Every surprise is deemed to be an intelligence failure. The attack on Europe's political capital has been widely blamed on bad intelligence and on the lack of information sharing among the many intelligence services of the European Union states. The EU has an enormous number of well-equipped states such as Great Britain and France to share intelligence and cross-border cooperation but trust is lacking among the European Union states.

Many nations are not willing to share intelligence with all the other EU nations due to a fear they may betray sources or undermine operations, resulting in less, rather than more cooperation. While the situation in Europe is not comparable to the United States, of course, the larger lesson of better integrating and coordinating across various policy fields that pertain to security does appear to be necessary in order to prevent future attacks.

As European Union states do not trust each other enough to share information, it is clear that intelligence work and defense are the responsibility of the individual member states. Intelligence expert Musa Khan Jalalzai has beautifully painted a true picture of EU intelligence cooperation at the law enforcement level, and he has also elucidated some important facts about the intelligence surveillance mechanisms of British agencies. This book will update all readers, and is a call to action for those attached to the intelligence information gathering, analysis and processing apparatus.

Introduction

Great minds discuss ideas; Average minds discuss events;
small minds discuss people. — Eleanor Roosevelt

In an increasingly globalized world, intelligence has become an ever more important weapon of the state. The impact of globalization on intelligence cooperation among the EU member states is rendered problematic by divergent conceptions of its nature and the contradictory expectations that have resulted. The recent developments in information technology as well as the war against terrorism are the main factors impelling states to increase intelligence cooperation. Undoubtedly, intelligence sharing and interoperability of information systems has been the biggest challenges facing the EU member states due to their reservation on sharing national secrets.

To fulfill and implement their counterterrorism plans, European states recognize the benefits of a collaborative and cooperative relationship between local intelligence and law enforcement agencies. Underscoring the critical role of these agencies, they have established several competent research institutions for the professionalization of intelligence information sharing, and understand that the joint operation of law enforcement personnel with intelligence counterparts can help to optimize the appropriate use of relevant intelligence information to support law enforcement investigations.

On some fronts, the EU faces obstacles to establishing a unified security network as every member state has its own priorities, resources and level of expertise when it comes to fighting terrorism. They are shy to share data and worry that their resources and methods might be exposed. Moreover, state intelligence agencies are also worried that mixing intelligence and law-enforcement information could lead to mistrials and procedural errors.

This reluctant cooperation among the intelligence and law enforcement agencies of the European Union member states prompted several law enforcement challenges. In his detailed analysis about the intelligence alliances and dangerous intelligence cooperation after the September 11 terrorist attacks in the United States, Richard Aldrich illustrates the gloomy picture of mistrust on policy-related intelligence information: "Perspectives on the inner working of intelligence alliances differ sharply. Some argue that clandestine agencies pursue national interests ruthlessly against friends and enemies alike. Established allies fight over policy-related intelligence, corroding trust and undermining possibilities for high-level policy convergence. One would hope that a sharing of intelligence among friends would promote similar outlook. But in reality, even the closest intelligence allies are reluctant to accept finished analysis from one another; turning instead to raw data for fear that they will become victims of analytical spin. Whether allies ultimately receive raw data or mere analysis is a function of their place in the intelligence hierarchy".[1]

The recent terrorist attacks in Belgium and France have once again highlighted the contradiction between the seemingly free movement of terrorists across Europe and the lack of EU-wide intelligence sharing. In fact, Edward Snowden's revelations (2013) were not limited to the United States Secret Surveillance Operations (USSSO); they also concern secret surveillance operations by the European intelligence agencies. The information leaked by Edward Snowden also confirmed the GCHQ's secret surveillance mechanism against British citizens. These

---

[1] *Dangerous Liaisons: Post September 11 Intelligence Alliances*, Richard Aldrich, *Harvard International Review* 06 September 2002.

revelations led to a considerable debate in print and electronic media, which highlighted the dangers of the agency's intrusive capabilities.

The basic function of intelligence surveillance mechanisms across the globe have appeared with different, contradictory shapes, which causes many challenges in society. In November 2015, the existence of a top secret program designed to spy on the British public was confirmed by UK Home Secretary Theresa May. The Home Secretary announced that MI5 spied on British citizens with the approval of the government, using bulk collection and analysis of citizens' personal data for more than 15 years.

Today's European societies face numerous challenges including radicalization, bioterrorism, and the failure of governments to adopt effective national security measures. Security experts suggest that a smooth and secure cross-border intelligence information exchange between the law enforcement agencies of all EU member states would be very effective in plugging the gaps in the professionalization of intelligence cooperation. EU policy makers view the consequences of the potential return of more than 5,000 jihadists to attack Europe as a bigger security challenge.

The issue of border checks also raised several questions such as watch lists, which are maintained poorly. The lack of up-to-date information has further prompted mutual misunderstanding. Guns and other firearms are still easily available in the streets and towns of all EU states, which makes it easier for terrorist groups to carry out attacks on public places. In the UK, the presence of thousands of criminal gangs, dozens of terrorist networks, and more than 400 war criminals, raises serious questions about the security measures of the law enforcement agencies of the country.

Since the EU special agencies are handled by different formal and informal entities, researchers are unable to show the whole picture in a broad perspective. When we read stories about state and private intelligence agencies, and their evolving functions, we come across numerous analyses and comments, which point to the role of private agencies as a bigger challenge for the state agencies in the EU. No doubt, the EU Intelligence Analysis

Centre (INTCEN) produces the best research reports and helps member states in professionalizing their intelligence infrastructure, but due to the lack of cooperation among member states all hopes of unity have vanished.

In fact, the EU Intelligence Centre (INTCEN) is part of the EEAS, and its role is to provide intelligence analysis, early warning, and situational awareness, but in 2015, it badly failed to positively respond to the prevailing terror culture within the European Union member states, particularly in France and Belgium. After the Paris and Brussels attacks of November 2015 and well into 2016, a new structure for the EU intelligence and security sector cooperation was demanded.

The migrant crisis also led to calls for increasing intelligence cooperation, information sharing and the establishment of a separate EU intelligence agency, but intelligence support for a vibrant foreign policy has failed to elicit the support of South and East Asian states in fighting radicalization and terrorism. In his intelligence analysis report, Director of the Greek Research Institute for European and American Studies Mr. John M. Nomikos stresses the need for a competent EU intelligence agency to counter the emerging threats of extremism, biochemical attacks, and nuclear terrorism within the perimeter of the European Union:

> Eventually, by establishing an intelligence service, Europe might be able to foresee a situation which could be threatening to the European Union States such as a crisis in the Balkans or prospective religious turmoil or biochemical attacks in Europe or Middle East/Gulf states to terrorist acts; Southern European Union member states such as Spain, Portugal, Italy and Greece are facing the effects of transnational crime and Muslim fundamentalism via illegal migration and human trafficking; the Council of Ministers should be involved as well by informing appropriately their national intelligence services. Since the Council of Ministers is the official decision-making body of the European Union, it should receive reports and analyses from the European Union intelligence service. However, the problem here

is that a Minister of Foreign Affairs might have difficulties and conflicts in dealing with the foreign affairs of his own country and that of the European Union at the same time. Of course, there are ways around this; for instance, the creation of a Committee on European Intelligence could refer directly to the European Union Commission.[1]

The United Kingdom did not react positively to the recent intelligence crisis and developed its own thesis that the weak European counter-terror efforts and poor data sharing cannot restore the confidence of all member states. The UK Foreign Minister remarked frankly and said that the EU lacks an effective intelligence mechanism. In an interview with the Financial Times, Mr. Hammond said: "Our intelligence agencies work seamlessly together. We don't talk about the different agencies in government—whether it is MI6, MI5, or GCHQ. We just talk about the single intelligence [output]. There are different legal structures, different powers, and often there are even turf wars, all of which reduce the operational effectiveness of [other countries' agencies] compared to ours," Mr. Hammond said.

Britain maintains a professional infrastructure of intelligence and surveillance mechanisms and collects every piece of intelligence information with care. The system of analysis and process are based on strongest security policies, strategies and law enforcement mechanisms. But unfortunately, 95% of the UK citizens have no basic knowledge of the function of dozens secret intelligence units of their country. One of these secret units is an Electronic Intelligence Unit (EIU) that is responsible for surveillance; and electronic propaganda campaigns focused on law enforcement and counterterrorism operations. However, the changing role of Joint Threat Research Intelligence Group (JTRIG) came under severe criticism from various social and political circles when Ms. Jo Cox, Labour MP, was killed by a terrorist in Birstall, in her Batley & Spen constituency (2016). The JTRIG is helping law enforcement agencies, including Met

---

[1] "The role of an intelligence service within the European Union Mechanism," John M. Nomikos, the Greek Research Institute for European and American Studies, 17 November 2013, Greece

Police, MI5, Revenue and Customs (HMRC), and the National Public Order and Intelligence Unit (NPOIU). Researchers Glenn Greenwald and Andrew Fishman (22 June 2015) have deeply analyzed the secret operational mechanism of this unit and elucidated many aspects of its evolving operational mechanism:

> Documents published by The Intercept demonstrate how the Joint Threat Research Intelligence Group (JTRIG), a unit of the Signals Intelligence Agency, Government Communications Headquarters (GCHQ), is involved in efforts against political groups it considers "extremist," Islamist activity in schools, the drug trade, online fraud and financial scams. Though its existence was secret until last year, JTRIG quickly developed a distinctive profile in the public understanding, after documents from NSA whistleblower Edward Snowden revealed that the unit had engaged in "dirty tricks" like deploying sexual "honey traps" designed to discredit targets, launching denial-of-service attacks to shut down Internet chat rooms, pushing veiled propaganda onto social networks and generally warping discourse online.[1]

The Washington Post and the Guardian published important stories on 13 June, 2013, about the information leaked by Edward Snowden which exposed the US and UK secret data gathering mechanism through PRISM, UPSTREAM and TEMPORA. After these revelations, the UK Intelligence and Security Committee (ISC) simply declared that the allegations that GCHQ had acted illegally by accessing the content of private communications via the PRISM program were "unfounded." In 2015, the ISC conducted inquiry into the capabilities of electronic intelligence in intrusive techniques. The Intelligence Committee concluded that the existing legal framework governing these capabilities was unnecessarily complicated, and recommended that it be replaced with a new Act of Parliament.

Edward Snowden exposed the GCHQ's secret intelligence operation and phone hacking power in his interview with BBC

---

[1] http://readersupportednews.org/news-section2/318-66/30883-british-documents-reveal-massive-domestic-spying

in October 2015. Mr. Snowden said that GCHQ gains access to a telephone set by sending it an encrypted text message and uses it for such things as taking pictures and listening in. Moreover, documents leaked by Edward Snowden also revealed details about the GCHQ operation inside Pakistan, where the agency has been secretly hacking into routers manufactured by the US company Cisco, BBC reported. Once the GCHQ gains access to a user's handset, the agency is able to view "who you are calling, what you texted, the things you've browsed, the list of your contacts, the places you've been, the wireless networks that your phone is associated with," Mr. Snowden said.

On 09 February 2016, in his Daily Dot article, Eric Geller noted the power mechanism of GCHQ in data collection within the matrix of the legal framework: "GCHQ can collect 'external' communications in bulk under a section 8(4) warrant. It can then search for and select communications to examine using a selector of an individual who is overseas, providing the Secretary of State has certified this as necessary for statutory purposes. If GCHQ wants to search for and select 'external' communications to examine based on a selector of an individual in the UK, they must get additional authorization from a Secretary of State which names that person. The Secretary of State cannot issue section 8(1) or section 8(4) warrants unless they believe it is both necessary and proportionate."[1]

Since the first disclosures by Edward Snowden in June 2013, a number of challenges to GCHQ's surveillance practices have been initiated in the UK. In response to one of those applications, the IPT court that oversees the GCHQ ruled against the UK intelligence services for the first time in its controversial 15 year history. Moreover, the IPT ruled: "the regime governing the soliciting, receiving, storing and transmitting by the UK authorities of private communications of individuals in the UK that were obtained the NSA's PRISM and UPSTREAM breached articles 8 and 10 of the European Convention for Human Rights."

There is speculation that if the reluctance for intelligence cooperation among EU states continues, British intelligence agen-

---

[1] On 09 February 2016, in his *Daily Dot* article, Eric Geller noted the power mechanism of GCHQ in data collection within the matrix of legal framework.

cies may possibly suffer huge damage. On 24 March 2016, the Guardian defense and intelligence correspondence, Mr. Ewan MacAskill, reported an intellectual debate focused on the counterterrorism and security implications of the UK leaving European Union:

> The Islamic State attacks on Brussels cruelly exposed the longstanding weaknesses and lack of cooperation between European spy agencies, opening the way for renewed arguments about whether the UK would be safer inside or out of the European Union. After the Paris attacks in November, there were promises by politicians in the UK, France, Germany, Belgium and elsewhere of increased cooperation but there has been no significant change," the newspaper reported.[1]

The UK, Germany, France, Poland and Netherlands intelligence agencies are professional and powerful, well-staffed, and efficient but others are shambolic or close to non-existent. Belgium's intelligence service is under-resourced and understaffed, with little cooperation between it and the myriad different police services. The Paris terrorist attacks in 2015, followed by the Copenhagen and Brussels terror attacks in 2016, quickly changed the perception of the professionalization of intelligence cooperation within the EU.

In all the EU member states, thousands of asylum seekers from South Asia, Afghanistan and the Arab world showing fake identity documents have claimed asylum, but their real identity is not known, nor do we know how many have military training or who financed their travel from the states where they live. At the same time, EU citizens who became radicalized and went to fight in Syria, Iraq and Afghanistan have returned with new ideologies, perceptions and resolves. In fact, the EU due to the lack of intelligence-sharing is under constant criticism. Britain presents the same tainted picture, where Muslim extremist and terrorist groups have established no-go areas across the country.

---

[1] "Would Brexit damage British intelligence?" Ewen MacAskill, *The Guardian*, 24 March 2016, http://www.theguardian.com/politics/2016/mar/24/brussels-brexit-really-undermine-the-uks-intelligence-capabilities.

The idea that all states should work for a common objective failed due to the lack of a common security policy. Europe's struggle to keep Britain in the project appears to have failed, while the major internal security threat and the fear of Russian aggression together with the refugee crisis will continue to cause problems. Before the Paris attacks, there were plans to enhance security cooperation among EU members, but their shifting priorities and reluctance to place joint security above national security has dimmed hopes. It is a very difficult task to bring into reality — much less to streamline — intelligence cooperation among member states.

In the wake of the Nice and Munich terrorist attacks in July 2016, community leaders and security experts raised several questions about the unprofessional approach of local law enforcement agencies. Then, on 07 August 2016, a machete-wielding man launched an attack outside the Belgian city Charleroi's main police station and left two Belgian officers injured as a third officer killed the man. He had hacked at a policewoman's face with his machete and shouted "Allahu Akbar" (God is Great) before turning on another officer. The attacker was shot in the chest and the leg. He was taken to hospital where he later died.

After these attacks, intelligence experts in France and Belgium admitted that their countries' agencies had failed to tackle radicalization and international terrorism. The fact of the matter is that neither France nor the EU member states have introduced professional intelligence reforms to design a comprehensive preventive strategy. A committee of lawmakers in a press conference regretted on the lack of coordination between the foreign and domestic intelligence agencies.

German intelligence is not so different from the French spy agencies. Most of the current intelligence problems within the European Union, as in Pakistan and India, whether they relate to predicting surprise attacks, the politicization of intelligence, or questions of ethics and privacy, are old conundrums. However, it is hard to escape the feeling that closer attention to obvious lessons from the past would have assisted the intelligence sharing of these states in avoiding the Taliban, ISIS and other ethnic and sectarian groups attacks on civilian and military installations.

After the London, Madrid, Paris, Munich and Nice attacks, the EU member states are still waiting for miracles to bring a readymade remedy to their pain. The most critical counter terrorism efforts within the project still need to be streamlined where law enforcement agencies have failed to share information properly.

Europol and Eurojust have also failed to deliver. The EU intelligence agencies complain that the Europol policing organization is unable to deliver, particularly in the field of investigation. Moreover, Europol has also failed to prove itself as a professional policing organization after the Paris and Germany attacks. One of the most important tasks of an intelligence agency is to investigate and provide immediate warning of foreign and domestic terrorist attacks during a spike in security threats in a given country.

One reason behind these failures is that intelligence and law enforcement agencies operate on opposite directions in a complex legal environment. There is a huge difference between these agencies over the conceptualization of the war against terrorism in Iraq, Syria and Afghanistan. Europol and Eurojust are confused and do not know how to operate in collaboration with all the EU intelligence agencies. Furthermore, the law enforcement and intelligence infrastructure of the EU's Eastern partners has raised many question including insecurity and Russia's political and military influence in this region. NATO is sending more troops and funds to the region, saying it needs to counter the Russian influence, but it is too late to win the heart and mind of the ruling elite of Ukraine, Georgia and Moldova who enjoy no security guarantee.

Europe is suffering due to the lack of coordination that could help identify and intercept terrorists before they carry out their attacks. There are so many things holding EU member states back from moving ahead with a single voice that some even speculate that the security assurance of all member states within the EU is mere hyperbole.

The Netherlands, Denmark, Moldova and the Baltic states feel threatened. Their recent complaints against the weak intelligence-sharing mechanism are of great concern. Professional intelligence and law enforcement approach is not something readymade; it must be painstakingly built by experts and policy makers. Since 2012, terrorists have carried out more than nine deadly attacks, in which 249 civilians were killed. They used different tactics, keeping the law enforcement agencies off balance.

The issue of security sector reforms in France and Germany is often discussed in print and electronic media, but in reality, their zeal and resolve are revolving around old mechanisms. More than 24 years ago, some intelligence reforms were introduced in France under the 1991 Law, and intelligence surveillance was confined to the tapping of wireless telephone communications. After that initiative, in 2015, an intelligence act was adopted by the French government, but after the terror attacks in 2015 and 2016, the country's parliamentary investigation identified multiple failures of French intelligence. The investigation later on recommended a fusion of all six intelligence agencies. Socialist lawmaker Sebastien Pietrasanta told journalists that two intelligence chiefs had admitted intelligence failure.

French Prime Minister Manuel Valls presented a package of immediate reforms on 21 January 2015 to address the issue of radicalization and terrorism in his country, but unfortunately, the new counterterrorism measures did not prove effective. These were seen as measures taken against Muslim communities and they have weakened the roots of French intelligence agencies; the lack of trust has further added to the country's pain. In these new intelligence efforts, the government has created a code of internal security within the Intelligence Act, which intends to create a climate of trust between intelligence agencies and ethnic minority communities. The Act stresses technical capabilities of the intelligence infrastructure to harmonize the range of tools that intelligence services can use according to the regime applicable to judicial investigations.

Before the terrorist attacks in Nice on Bastille Day, 14 July 2016, the failure of French intelligence was mainly due to its lack of coordination with law enforcement agencies. However, when these summer killings started, police and security agencies were unable to react promptly or intercept the truck immediately. All these attacks were carried out under the police and intelligence surveillance system, which means something is going wrong under the carpet.

The Chief of the French domestic intelligence warned in June that terrorist attacks were inevitable. In these circumstances, French law makers had no option other than to call for a shake-up of the intelligence infrastructure. Likewise, the consecutive failure of German intelligence agencies to intercept lone wolves and Muslim extremists before they translate their resentment into a violent action has raised important questions. This lack of predictable security management is a focus of debate today.

The former Soviet republics of Moldova and Georgia are suffering both a security crisis and political fragmentation. Moldova is not entirely onboard with EU integration, while Georgian citizens are troubled by the fact that they still face an uneven visa regime within EU member states. Meanwhile, even, German intelligence has spied on France, and created clouds of surveillance on US and Britain, while Britain spied on Germany, which engendered distrust. Already in 2013, the BBC was reporting that the head of the German parliament's intelligence committee had called for enquiries into alleged spying committed by the British embassy in Berlin. German intelligence agencies are looking at the US and UK through a hostile lens after Angela Merkel's personal telephone was tapped by NSA and the UK's illegal surveillance operation in the country.

And lastly, Britain's decision to leave the EU could have a significant impact on the Union's ability to help nations to the east in implementing political and economic reform or to respond to Russia's continued influence in the region.

Finally, I would like to thank Algora Publishing and the editors for their sincere cooperation and guidance, and my friends Afghan lawyer Mr. Meftahuddin Haroon, independent researcher and columnist Mr. Noor Dahri, and PhD candidate Mrs. Diva Patang Wardak, who helped me in finding valuable books and open source intelligence reports.

Musa Khan Jalalzai
August 2016, London

CHAPTER 1. FIXING THE EU INTELLIGENCE CRISIS

Knowledge will forever govern ignorance; and a people
who mean to be their own governors must arm themselves with
the power which knowledge gives. — *James Madison*

The European Union (EU) is a community of different nations with different perceptions, ideologies, cultures, ways of life, and ways of maintaining a balance between domestic and international policies. Recently, new perceptions and ideologies of partnership developed that pushed some states to the wall. Their inner pain and political discrimination inculcates them that the Americanized counterterrorism strategies, policies and way of fighting against radicalization and terrorism is no more effective, because they believe their own culture of peace, law enforcement, and security can bring stability to the region. As the US counterterrorism strategies in Middle East, Persian Gulf and South Asia caused controversies and suspicions, the EU member states also lost confidence due to their cooperation in killings and torture with the United States army and agencies.[1]

The EU states are committed to protect the union with a

---

[1] "Still waters run deep: the EU Intel crisis", *Daily Times*, 15 March, 2016, also, "The European Union and the Member States: two different perceptions of border," Teresa Ciercol, Jorge Tavares da Silva, Rev. bras. polit. int. vol.59 no.1 Brasília 2016 Epub, May 24, 2016, http://www.scielo.br/scielo.php?script=sci_arttext&pid=S0034-73292016000100203

common counterterrorism mechanism, intelligence sharing, and foreign policy, but unfortunately, some states want to maintain their political and economic influence, and dictate the EU project along different lines. There are four categories of states that maintain their own priorities and perceptions of national security mechanism. Germany, France, Britain and Netherlands are powerful and influential states.[1] They have established strong and professional intelligence infrastructures, which collect national security related intelligence information and share with their allies to counter radicalization and extremism within the parameters of their EU project.

The information they receive from the weak EU states is neither professional nor effective in countering terrorism and radicalization. They complain that they don't need this kind of low-quality information, which cannot be used in policy making. The growing power of Russia and China, military developments in the Middle East, shifting terrain in South and Central Asia, and the turbulence of North Africa—all these factors call for a well-established professional intelligence agency within the EU perimeter. The establishment of such a common agency will improve the process of intelligence sharing among all member states.[2]

No doubt, EU counter terrorism strategies are based on cultural and social principles, but recent violent acts of terrorism in Norway France, Brussels, and Britain raised important questions about the weak security measures of the European Union member states. Civil War in Iraq, Afghanistan, Yemen, Libya, Syria and Pakistan has put under strain the whole security infrastructure of the region as hundreds professional criminals and terror elements entered the region. The arrival of thousands refugees from Africa and the Arab world with their sectarian affiliation further jeopardized the peaceful environment of European continent.[3]

The Paris and Brussels attacks in November 2015 raised serious questions about the ineffectiveness of Europe's Schengen

---

[1] "The European Union: Foreign and Security Policy," Derek E. Mix, April 8, 2013, *Congressional Research Service*
[2] *Daily Times*, 15 March 2016.
[3] Ibid.

Agreement, which allows passport-free travel between 26 European countries. The recent killings in France and Belgium also proved that terror elements returned from the battlefields of Asia and Africa can anytime disrupt the security infrastructure of the region. The emergence of Sectarianized and ethnicized mind and thought in various European states, specifically, in the United Kingdom and France, forced these two nations to introduce new surveillance laws and strategies to tackle the issue by technical means, but extremists and sectarian elements want to accomplish their religious and political agenda through violent means.[1]

Anti-terror legislation in the EU has traditionally evolved in response to events: urgent measures, like the European Arrest Warrant and the setting up of Eurojust (the Union's agency for judicial co-operation) were taken after the 9/11 attacks. Then in the wake of the Madrid and London bombings, in 2005, the EU adopted its first-ever counter-terrorism strategy. That was followed in 2006 by the so-called data retention directive, which required communication providers to store data about their customers for up to two years. However the European Court of Justice (ECJ) recently declared this directive void, stating that its provisions violated the EU rights of privacy and data protection.[2]

Terror related incidents in Britain and the recent attack in France diverted the attention of European Union policy makers to the point that home-grown extremist groups needed to be put under strict surveillance. What agenda Muhammad Merah wanted to accomplish in France is not known, but one thing is clear: he was brainwashed outside France. In France, military forces and police are "everywhere" since 7 January 2015, when the terrorist attack on Charlie Hebdo took place. French Prime Minister Manuel Valls said that 122,000 law enforcement personnel were tasked with the protection of the French population. The Ministry of Defense decided to deploy 10,500 soldiers to sensitive areas, with nearly half of them assigned to the protection of the country's seven hundreds seventeen Jewish schools.[3]

---

[1] *BBC* 07 March 2016
[2] *Report on Eurojust's Casework* in the Field of the Arrest Warrant, 2013. 2014.
[3] Ibid.

Other European nations also felt danger and started arresting individuals related to terror networks. In Germany, Netherlands, Norway and Britain, the same reaction was shown. There are numerous terror networks operating in the region. The PKK, BLA, Taliban, al Qaeda, Lashkar-e-Toiba, Afghani, and Pakistani, Bangladeshi extremist groups, Boko Haram, Al Shabab and many other extremist and sectarian groups are operating with their own agendas in Britain, France and Netherlands. According to some recent reports, PKK is a mafia group that runs the business of drug and arm trafficking. A recent US report termed PKK as an octopus-like structure carrying out criminal activity, including drug and people smuggling to raise funds and provide cover to the group terror networks across Europe.

The PKK also has a vast European propaganda machine and fundraising network which includes four television channels, two agencies, thirteen radio channels and dozens newspapers and periodicals. Pakistani Lashkar-e-Toiba, Somalian Al Shabab, Afghani Taliban and Nigerian Boko Haram have their own secret networks in Europe and the United Kingdom. They collect millions Pounds every year from business communities. French Interior Ministry announced the deportation of five Muslim extremists on 02 February, 2012. Police and counter terrorism authorities admit that these and other groups maintain more than 85 terrorist networks across the UK.

Germany's Justice Minister Heiko Maas argued that going to terrorist camps is a punishable offence. Here, the German government relied on a UN Resolution from September 2015 on foreign fighters. Firstly, extremists who seek to leave Germany to participate in "acts of violent subversion" abroad or to train for participation in such acts would be liable to prosecution in the future. Second, a new criminal offence he said for terrorism financing was also underway in Germany. The violent aftermath of the Arab spring provided a new motivation and new opportunities for extremists all over Europe, and militancy in Belgium itself was already broadening and deepening. One well-known, ostensibly non-violent, group of activists — Sharia4Belgium — that was responsible for a stream of aggressive hate-speech and alleged recruitment was eventually broken up.[1]

The question is, experts say, deportation is not the solution; the solution is to bring some changes in foreign and internal policies, and introduce an effective law of tolerance and race relations. What Europol has done so for and how it deals with the issues of extremism in Europe is the main question. Europol uses the information of its informers and experts to identify terror networks in Europe, but the way it wants to track terrorist has not been successful in the past. The intelligence networks of various states do not co-operate with each other in a proper way. They do not provide all necessary information to each other agencies. The way, Euro law enforcement agencies and Europol's Operational Coordination Centre and Secure Information Centre carry out more than 12,000 cross border investigations each year is no more effective. Terror and extremist networks are there, PKK is there, Al Qaeda is there, and Boko Haram is very much there.

The other ways of sharing information include; First Response Network, European Explosive Ordinance Disposal Network and the Euro Bomb Data System have produced no fruitful result. The latest TE-SAT Report revealed that terrorism continues to impact the lives of Euro citizens. France is under threat from extremist networks, because of the country's recent hostile policies and law against the Muslim veil in schools. French citizens have travelled to war zones and taken part in civil wars in Africa and Asia, received training from terrorist and extremist organizations and returned to their country with new and dangerous ideas, new sects and new messages. Upon their return, they have applied their skills and encouraged others to follow their violent ways. The threat of extremism is still real in Netherlands.[2]

The issue of race relations in the country is more complicated. Racism has created more problems for the law enforcement agencies of the country. Jihadist recruitments in Netherlands over the past few years have proved that extremist and terror groups have roots in the country. The nature of the ter-

---

[1] "How Belgium became a breeding ground for international terrorists," Jason Burke-16-11-2015
[2] *Daily Outlook*, 05 April 2012.

ror threat in Netherlands and other European states do reflect the struggle of home-grown extremist groups seeking to carry out attacks in various states, target government installation and religious places. In Afghanistan and Pakistan, all European extremist groups have representation in Taliban networks. A year ago, German extremist networks had the representation of two hundred fighters.

As of the beginning of 2013, the Netherlands intelligence (AIVD) noticed a number of Dutch jihadists leaving for Syria. Presently, the AIVD estimates 160 Dutch jihadists in the Syria/Iraq area. Within the jihadist movement in the Netherlands, the AIVD acknowledges a few hundred potential participants and several thousands of sympathizers. Netherlands General Intelligence and Security Service (AIVD), National Coordinator for Security and Counterterrorism (NCTV) have recently painted the transmogrified face of Salafism in a detailed report, which inculcates readers about the networks of the sect across the country:

> The Salafist movement in the Netherlands is organized to a limited extent, with structures representing its political and its apolitical strands. As well as controlling their own places of worship and charitable foundations, these currents also exert influence within the administrative bodies of other mosques. Close contacts between sections of the movement here in the Netherlands and Salafist individuals and structures in the Middle East potentially give those external players an (undesirable) level of influence over parts of the Dutch spectrum. Missionary work and mobilization activities also take place outside the established "Salafist centers." Moreover, many of those who attend Salafist lectures and sermons do not confine their religious loyalties to a single mosque or preacher. As well as centers with a more or less "official" identity, there are also "independent" preachers who organize meetings throughout the country, mainly aimed at young people. There is a huge amount of material available on the internet, too. Meanwhile, the jihadi Salafist strand operates outside

these formal structures. Thus, on the organizational level the Salafist spectrum is also very diverse.[1]

In February 2011, a French newspaper published classified documents of the country's counter intelligence agency which revealed the existence of 100 European nationals in the Pak-Afghan border area. Out of those 100 Europeans, 14 were French while citizens of Italy and Belgium were also receiving military training there. European police reported the arrival of more than 700,000 radicalized people in Europe from Afghanistan, Pakistan, Iran, Iraq, the Maghreb, Syria, West Bank, Gaza, Sudan, Nigeria, Egypt, Yemen and Somalia. In Sweden, there are more extremists who actively support terrorism in other states, through various means.[2]

As we read in newspapers and books, the current European societies face numerous challenges including radicalization, extremism, international terrorism and racism, the lack of coordination among their policing institutions, and the inattention of governments to adopt an effective national security measures, vulnerability and insecurity have badly affected their daily lives and businesses. Security experts suggest that a smooth and secure cross border intelligence information exchange between the law enforcement agencies of all EU member states can be very effective in fixing these challenges. When we read stories about the cross-border cooperation mechanism of EU states, we find intelligence cooperation on law enforcement level has less developed, and a range of obstacles have made cooperation cumbersome and still pose challenges.[3]

In fact, EU intelligence cooperation is still a dream as all member states are not willing to share their national secrets with each other and every state views the others with deep suspicion. Things got worse when Britain threatened to leave the Union if professional reforms were not introduced. Denmark, Spain, Greece and Sweden were in a deep crisis due to growing jihadism and internal security threats challenging the authority of their states. They also complained that they received

---

[1] Ibid.
[2] *Daily Times*, 15 March 2016.
[3] Ibid.

no intelligence sharing package from the EU agencies. The US also wanted Britain in, to protect the partnership of the EU in a global war on terrorism. The return of the Taliban and their exponentially growing networks across Afghanistan, the emergence of Islamic State (ISIS), and the unending war in the Middle East and Persian Gulf regions, have raised serious questions about the credibility and professional intelligence approach of EU intelligence agencies.[1]

The EU states need to fight radicalization and home-grown extremism, and put in place strategies to share intelligence on these issues. The root causes of radicalization are complex. Disaffection, lack of self-worth, poverty and discrimination all play a role. Researcher Simond de Galbert has warned:

> The frontier between the internal and external dimensions of the threat has essentially disappeared. About 5,000 EU citizens have travelled to Iraq and Syria as foreign terrorist fighters (FTFs). Many of them have already returned or will do so. Their EU citizenship makes it extremely difficult to track their movements within and outside of the Union. As illustrated by a March 1 report of the EU counterterrorism coordinator, this situation requires better coordination of member states' policies, first within the Union, second at its external borders, and third outside of the Union either for cooperation with third states or for intensifying the fight against the Islamic State in Syria and Iraq.[2]

The publication of the EU Council report on foreign terrorists spelled out the policy of member states against terrorism. After the Paris attacks, French and Belgian law-enforcement was unable to apprehend some of the attackers—despite clear warnings. The EU intelligence community is in deep crisis. The community encompasses national and European actors. National actors include national intelligence services, national security services, and police organizations. The actors in the field of intelligence are comprised on European information agencies (IN-

---

[1] Ibid.
[2] Simond de Galbert, in a research paper for the Center for Strategic and International Studies, 28 March 2016.

TDIV EUMS, SitCen, Europol, and EUSC). All these intelligence and surveillance agencies have seen a growing role of European information bodies. European bodies have always played a role in crisis management operations. Simond de Galbert noted that intelligence sharing is not a difficult task but it is variable. He, however, deferred the establishment of an EU intelligence agency, and said it is ill-advised:

> Intelligence sharing will always be easier on a bilateral basis, and it is fair to say that intelligence capabilities and contributions are highly variable across the Union. The idea of a European intelligence agency is therefore attractive but ill-advised in the current circumstances. Europeans' energy, resources, and political capital should be focused on realistic and pragmatic improvements—including legal ones as necessary—to the European Union's current framework.[1]

The difficulties of Intelligence-Sharing are administrative hurdles and reluctance to share national intelligence with another state. In order to prevent future terror attacks like those in Paris and Brussels, European nations need to cooperate on security issues. The international threat of terrorism thus requires a collective European response. Without bilateral exchanges, there would be no European intelligence cooperation at all. Overall, these contacts manage themselves. The bilateral contacts need little stimulation from the European level to yield good results for all parties involved.

The intelligence war among NATO and EU intelligence agencies, and their monitoring campaign against Chinese, Russian, Pakistani, Iranian and Indian agencies, make things worse as they are blaming each other for the failure of state and government in Afghanistan and Iraq. The mistrust between large and small states' intelligence expertise is a bigger problem. Strong and large states with their professional intelligence agencies oppose radical changes in the current intelligence sharing mechanism. Indian and Pakistani intelligence agencies (RAW and ISI) are deeply involved in proxy war, and in an intelligence war

---

[1] Ibid.

with CIA, MI6, AIVD and NDS in Afghanistan.

However, in the EU, small and weak states without professional agencies are unable to provide vital information to the large states. Now large states want to establish a joint mechanism on intelligence sharing, without the inclusion of small states. Disagreement between small and large states over the strategic relationship with the US has left a negative impact on the effectiveness of the EU. The US views terrorism as an external threat, while the EU member states view it as an internal threat.

Intelligence cooperation within the EU is of greater importance in fighting the threat of terrorism and radicalization, but the EU intelligence analysis centre (INTCEN) has nothing to offer as majority of member states intelligence agencies are competing for resources and attention from policy makers. Moreover, the INTCEN has no formal mandate to collect intelligence as traditionally understood, because the centre mostly depends on open source intelligence (OSINT). In 2012, INTCEN tried to improve its intelligence analysis capabilities and focus on analysis with two divisions; analysis division, and general and external relations divisions, but the case still remains weak. The issue of electronic intelligence generated numerous controversies within the member states. Privacy international and other organizations deeply criticized the way EU member states spy on their citizens.[1]

The EU confirms that The Charter of Foundation Rights and the European Convention for the protection of Human Rights and Fundamental Freedoms guarantee the right of privacy and personal data protection to everyone within the perimeter of the union, but if we look at the rising voices in European capitals against the offensive surveillance and violation of privacy, we come to the conclusion that all the claims of the EU member states about the protection of privacy are just for show, which is tantamount to their self defeat. During the operation of large scale electronic surveillance, citizens of EU member states consider that their right to privacy is being violated, and there is no balance between the needs of law enforcement and fundamental

[1] Ibid.

rights and privacy, personal data protection and family life. The Netherlands, Britain, Sweden, France and Germany are deeply involved in mass surveillance operations against their citizens.

On 18 December 2015, during the EU summit, all leaders promised to improve the process of intelligence sharing and fight against terrorism, but experts still wait to experiment a good reform package. The speed in which the EU intelligence sharing process developed meant that it has not yet a smooth ride. In March 2016, after the Brussels attacks, the EU Justice and Interior Ministers vowed to deepen joint intelligence gathering and swiftly push through measures to share airline passenger information and step up the fight against terrorism.

"We don't need new plans, we need to fully implement the plans and measures that have been taken," said Interior Minister Ronald Plasterk of the Netherlands, Brussels is not the only EU capital to face criticism. "There is a lack of trust, otherwise things might have been predicted and then prevented," said European Home Affairs Commissioner Dimitris Avramopoulos.[1]

CHAPTER 2. THE FAILURE OF EU INTELLIGENCE COOPERATION

The failure of French and Brussels intelligence agencies to tackle the menace of radicalization and the exponentially growing networks of the Islamic State (ISIS) prompted deep distrust between the law enforcement agencies and civil society of the two countries. European Union is in deep crisis, and the crisis of intelligence cooperation is exacerbated by the day, which causes the climate of distrust and fear across the continent. In the wake of the terrorist attacks in Brussels, security and intelligence experts raised the question of intelligence failure. On 22 March 2016, terrorists killed more than 34 innocent people and injured hundreds in the Belgium capital. The attacks highlighted systemic challenges; EU intelligence has failed to stem the tide of radicalization through proper integration and cooperation on the law enforcement level. The intelligence failure related to the Paris terrorist attacks were more serious than the intelligence failure in Brussels, where terrorists and radicalized elements openly dance in the streets with impunity.[1]

Normally, intelligence failure occurs due to preventable conditions, by which I mean a lack of coordination, cooperation and poor distribution of intelligence among the relevant agencies of the European Union member states. To prevent intelligence

---

[1] *France-24*, 22 March 2016.

failure, intercourse between the three level of intelligence (strategic, operational and tactical) is necessary. Intelligence failure can be broadly defined as a misunderstanding of the prevailing situation or a developing breakdown of law and order. The issue has been very complex within the EU member states as they all lack a coordinated counterterrorism strategy and intelligence sharing system.[1]

There are over a dozen intelligence and law enforcement agencies supporting the EU security, but several of them lack professional demonstration. In fact, the EU needs a new national security approach, a new intelligence analysis and cooperation approach. The present national security and intelligence dissemination approach is weak, unprofessional and disorganized. As we have seen in the past, several intelligence failures in the European Union occurred due to the lack of adequate data, dearth of trained agents, the wrong way of the application of surveillance technology, intelligence sharing, lack of action, and the lack of sensible intelligence reforms. In the aftermath of the terrorist attacks in France and Belgium, the EU intelligence agencies and their way of cooperation remained in question. In his research paper "Why Intelligence Fails,"[2] Indian scholar Janani Krishnaswamy describes some important aspects of intelligence failure and its causes:

> The source of intelligence failure resides not only within the boundaries of the intelligence procedures but also in the inaction of the policy makers to react on the intelligence made available, the intelligence community's inability to adapt to the changing faces of terror, and the reform makers failure to make appropriate proposals of intelligence reforms.......The story of intelligence reform is far from complete. Even if some reforms were sensible in fixing a few troubles of the intelligence community, reform makers have not been able to mend the core predicaments of the community because of (a) a failure to make any post event audit, (b) lack of

---

[1] *Daily Times*, 24 March 2016.
[2] In *Policy Report No. 3*, The Hindu Centre for Politics and Public Policy, 2013.

professionalism and systematized functioning, (c) communication gap between procedures and consumers of intelligence, and lack of protocol for engaging and de-engaging, (d) failure to implement reforms to recruit and train intelligent personnel, (e) failure to improve the working of intelligence personnel and, (f) and failure to adequately strengthen local intelligence.[1]

The issue of intelligence cooperation in the EU now became the centre of debate in international forums that without intelligence sharing on law enforcement level, terrorism and violent extremism cannot be countered. Monica Den Boer (22 Jan 2015) noted the function of EU intelligence and security agencies in a research paper:

> The bulk of international counter-terrorism activity is still performed in the bilateral sphere between the individual member states of the EU, as well as in networked arrangements which are not subjected to formal accountability rules. Counter-terrorism measures have undergone a steep rise since the 9/11 attacks in the United States. The EU Member States themselves placed considerable emphasis on security measures and the speed of the adoption meant there was little room for alternative voices to be heard. A decade after 9/11, there seems to be more room for reflection and for the argument that the efficiency of intelligence-exchange for the purpose of counter-terrorism will be best served if it is done professionally, proportionately, legally and brought under the realms of sound control and oversight. The EU is a collective actor in the sense that its institutions and its agencies carry a joint responsibility for intelligence. In this context, it plays the role of facilitator, exchequer, coordinator, owner, analyst and provider.[2]

---

[1] *Policy Report*-III, "Why Intelligence Fails," Janani Krishnaswamy, The Hindu Centre for Politics and Public Policy, India, 2013.
[2] *Counter-Terrorism, Security and Intelligence in the EU: Governance Challenges for Collection, Exchange and Analysis*, Monica Den Boer, 22 Jan 2015.

Authors of a recent paper on intelligence cooperation have also painted a useful picture of intelligence cooperation among the EU member states: "The development of a guide on accountability of international cooperation is a challenging but important undertaking. At least four reasons make this guide relevant for overseers and other interested parties: (1) the significant and ongoing increase in the breadth and depth of international intelligence cooperation, (2) the need to provide overseers with a practical guide on how they can go about holding intelligence services and the executive to account for international intelligence cooperation; (3) to assess how the risks of international intelligence cooperation, in particular risks for human rights and the rule of law, can be addressed through accountability; and (4) to provide guidance on the legal framework under which international intelligence cooperation occurs.[1]

In general, the benefits of organizing intelligence work at the multilateral level are fairly straightforward. From a strict intelligence perspective, there are obvious gains from cooperation related to economies of scale, specialization and diminishing transaction costs measured in money as well as time. For example, expensive technological systems such as satellites could be funded jointly, interpretation of specialist foreign tongues could be divided to avoid duplication and overlaps in capacity and time-sensitive information could be quickly shared with several national agencies through one central hub rather than an array of bilateral channels. To these generic intelligence gains one might add the political gains of multilateral intelligence cooperation.

The growing importance of cooperation emphasizes the second reason why this guide has been drafted: to fulfill an increasing need for specific guidance on how accountability and oversight of international intelligence cooperation can be strengthened on the basis of practical examples. Indeed, international intelligence cooperation is a challenging subject for overseers, and various characteristics of international intelligence cooperation can in some respects threaten or undermine the accountability processes. The EU intelligence system largely depends on

---

[1] *Making International Intelligence Cooperation Accountable, Hans Born, Ian Leigh, Aidan Wills, DCA21, May 2015 EU Home Affairs Agencies and the Construction of EU Internal Security*, Joanna Parkin, 2012.

member state contributions. How are the differences in member state resources and intelligence power accommodated in this common system? While formal equality among states is a basic tenet of EU affairs, this is not the case in intelligence affairs.

In the case of structured international intelligence cooperation, some form of hierarchy might be a precondition for the participation of powerful states. Every EU member state has its own domestic law enforcement and intelligence agencies that maintain law and order and counter terrorism and radicalization. One cannot claim that these agencies share their intelligence information or not, one thing is clear that without their cooperation security cannot be maintained within the matrix of the EU. Researcher Joanna Parkin has noted some important facts relating to the function and operation of these agencies:

> The EU's new Internal Security Strategy now takes this development one step further by integrating agency generated strategic analysis products and intelligence tools into political priority setting and decision-making within the ISS . . . As Radaelli noted in his study of expert knowledge in European public policy, "knowledge enters the policy process in combination with interests, never alone." The nature and purposes of agency-generated knowledge therefore call for closer attention and reflection. Agencies such as Frontex have substantial research budgets and large departments dedicated to R&D and 'data-gathering'. They are also responsible for the large-scale proliferation of 'knowledge' on security threats facing the EU via the regular publication of 'policy tools' such as threat assessments, risk analyses, periodic and situation reports. Eurojust also undertakes a form of research project titled 'Strategic projects'. One such project, focusing on 'Enhancing the work of Eurojust in drug trafficking cases' analyzed and evaluated data and outcomes of Eurojust coordination meetings on drug trafficking cases between 1st September 2008 and 31st August 2010, to identify the main challenges and solutions concerning drug trafficking cases identified in Eurojust's work. The project's final report incorporates discussions at a so-called 'strategic seminar' in Krakow and the results of casework analysis.

Hence, some cooperation has been described as a form of "subcontracted intelligence collection based on barter." The relative significance of information provided by foreign partners as a method of collection depends inter alia on a service's own collection capabilities and the subject matter. Small and medium-sized states generally rely extensively on larger partners for their information. Yet even states with major intelligence capabilities have gaps in their coverage and can benefit from receiving information from foreign services.[1]

In some cases, intelligence relations with particular states and groups, such as terrorist organizations, are not aligned with publicly declared foreign relations. Governments may use intelligence relationships to pursue goals that are not publicly acknowledged. The secretive nature of international intelligence cooperation provides an opportunity for relations with services from states with which a service's government may not have close or any diplomatic relationships. The pre-1994 relationship between Israel and Jordan is a good example.[2]

A majority of the causal factors identified in Western theories advanced earlier are extremely useful in explaining intelligence failures, no matter where they have happened. However, none—to the best of my knowledge—has dealt with the failure of intelligence review committees in advancing narrow theoretical treatments in explaining failures. Western scholars have formulated theories about what causes intelligence failures and also explain how to destroy these causes. However, the root cause of the various failures of the intelligence community in India predominantly exists in the failure to sufficiently understand such causes......Universally, it is accepted that intelligence failures arise only when analytic judgments of intelligence analysts turn out to be imprecise in a big way or when a major surprise occurs because of inadequate or imprecise intelligence warning.[3]

In the contemporary international marketing and business world, digital intelligence is also of great importance. Every year,

[1] Ibid.
[2] *Why Intelligence Fails*, Janani Krishnaswamy, Policy Report No. 3 2013, The Hindu Centre for Politics and public Policy, Policy Report No-3, 2013
[3] *Understanding Digital Intelligence and the Norms that Might Govern It*, David Omand, 2015, the Centre for International Governance Innovation and Chatham House

kicks off with a broader view on where marketers are focusing their attention. The interaction between government and law enforcement for digital intelligence demand, and the new possibilities that digital technology has opened up for meeting such demands is a good development. The adequacy of previous regimes of legal powers and governance arrangements is seriously challenged just at a time when the objective need for intelligence on the serious threats facing civil society is apparent. Professor David Omand's recent research paper elucidated the importance and demand of digital intelligence:

> Most security and intelligence authorities see themselves as having a duty to seek and use information, including digital intelligence, to help manage threats to public and national security. Secret intelligence, because it involves overcoming the determined efforts of others, such as terrorists, to prevent it being acquired, inevitably involves running moral hazard such as collateral intrusion upon privacy of those such as family members who may be entirely innocent. Like law enforcement at the start of an investigation, it is also often necessary to examine a number of witnesses to a crime or associates of suspects in order to eliminate them from enquiries. The examination of those later shown to be innocent of wrongdoing is an inevitable consequence of investigative law enforcement. It should also be recognized that the powerful tools of digital intelligence are already being used in some repressive non-democratic countries for censorship and control of dissidents.[1]

The case of EU intelligence failure is very complex as member states hardly understand the process of transforming information into intelligence an easy task, while in reality it needs professional demonstration and mature mechanism. As we experienced intelligence failure in Iraq and Afghanistan and its

---

[1] On 23 March 2016, *Sputnik International* reported Mr. Anton Tsvetkov, a Russian security official and director of the organization of Russian officers, suggested: "In such cases all the law enforcement services are put on high alert; the security of the entire strategic and transport infrastructure is intensified and the major purpose of the intelligence services is to prevent repeated attacks."

frightening consequences, the EU states need to learn more from the US failed strategies in Iraq and Afghanistan to streamline their intelligence sharing and counterterrorism efforts. Terror attacks in Paris and Brussels proved the failure of intelligence. Some security analysts understand that terrorists had planned to attack the nuclear installation of Belgium but dropped it because one of their colleagues was arrested.

On 01 April 2016, the Giancarlo Elia Valori report noted some evidence that the ISIS terrorist network in Brussels had planned a dirty bomb attack:

> On November 30, 2015, the Belgian police discovered a film regarding the movements of a Belgian nuclear researcher and his family who operated in Dohel-1, one of the seven nuclear production sites in that country, four in the Dohel region and three in the Tihange region. The long film of all the nuclear expert's movements was found in the Auvelais house of a man linked to the network of Al Baghdadi's Caliphate. The jihadists were interested not so much in the nuclear plant as such, but in the possibility of using radioisotopes, namely products capable of causing poisonings, diseases, and various temporary or permanent disorders in those who come into contact with them for a certain period of time. Radioisotopes, also known as radionuclides, are unstable nuclei which radioactively decay, resulting in the emission of nuclear radiations. As already said, the effects may be scarcely or highly significant, depending on the dose of radiations received and/or the type of emissions absorbed.[1]

If we look at the intelligence operation of some EU member states, we can quickly assess the causes of their success and failure. The Belgium Law enforcement had failed to deliver when terrorists started killing innocent civilians. Anton Tsvetkov, a Russian security official and director of the organization of Russian officers, suggested: "In such cases all the law enforcement services are put on high alert; the security of the entire strategic

---

[1] Giancarlo Elia Valori report (Modern Diplomacy, 2016).

and transport infrastructure is intensified and the major purpose of the intelligence services is to prevent repeated attacks. The second objective is to identify and detain all those involved in masterminding and executing the attack. When a terrorist attack has already happened or even when there is a person walking with a bomb along the street—it already represents a serious failure of the Special Forces."[1]

The French and Belgium intelligence infrastructure suffered from a lack of check and balance and the consumer hardly get what they need. The oversight system is weak, if we look at the oversight system of US, UK and Australia, we can find how it works and how they manage the professionalization level of intelligence mechanism. The case of Belgian is quite different. The Belgian law enforcement agencies are struggling to counter terrorism without well reformed intelligence agencies. Huge intelligence gap has badly affected the intelligence cooperation with other EU member states. Brussels intelligence became under scrutiny, while the EU member states are in compunction on their reluctance of intelligence sharing.

As the looming threat of dirty bomb or nuclear terrorism is causing torment and fear within the European Union member states, or as terrorist organizations are struggling to obtain dirty bomb materials to attack government and civilian installations in Europe, the Giancarlo Elia Valori report (2016) paints a new picture of nuclear terrorism in the region:

> The transition from the old to the new jihad, which came to maturity with the establishment of the Daesh-ISIS Caliphate, has already changed this Islamist strategic project on Europe. This is exactly the reason why we must be very careful with nuclear "dirty bombs" that will certainly reach their political goal (which is what matters), regardless of their actual potential for nucleotide radiation. Fear is a mechanism which now increases also with small doses of violence. It is hard to estimate how many sites exist today in the world where radionuclides are produced and stored, but the best statistics now available point to over 70,000 storage sys-

---

[1] 23 March 2016, *Sputnik International*.

tems placed in at least 13,000 facilities. The brutality of the attacks and the size of the widespread jihadist network discovered so far in Belgium may be explained by the fact that this country is one of the major world producers of radionuclides and there is at least one re-searcher of Islamic origin and faith who works in this facility, as we will see shortly. It is the nuclear complex called SK-CEN, a nuclear research centre located near the Bocholt-Herentals Canal, 53 miles away from Brus-sels. It no longer receives the periodical shipments of radioactive material from the United States, which in 2004 had reported the poor defense structures of the Belgian system in view of a possible attack by Al Qaeda.[1]

Over the last 15 years, growing national security controver-sies mostly revolved around the failure of cooperation among the European Union (EU) member states, which resulted in mistrust and the emergence of major extremist organizations that threatened the national security of the region. Cooperation among EU intelligence agencies failed to cultivate a strong re-lationship with policymakers and a close interaction with the civil society. Their sharp criticism against each other points to an important question about the border security and immigra-tion crisis in the region. However, amidst this controversial en-gagement, German intelligence spied on France and created the clouds of surveillance on US and Britain. On November 6, 2013, the BBC reported that the head of German parliament's intel-ligence committee called for enquiries into alleged spying com-mitted by the British embassy in Berlin.[2]

The German Home Minister asked the UK ambassador to explain his embassy's activities. This controversial way of intel-ligence sharing and cooperation has embroiled the EU member states in the biggest crisis of integration as several states have threatened to drag back their blankets. The Greek, Portuguese, Italian and Spanish financial crises further increased their pain. The political goal of creating a unified EU also failed as France

---

[1] *The Guardian*, 18 December 2015
[2] On February 11, 2016, Eric King, a visiting professor of law at Queen Mary University London, criticized the UK government's new Investigatory Powers Bill and raw intelligence sharing mechanism.

and Germany started dictating their partner states. Thus, the proposals of forming a common EU intelligence agency caused controversies, and raised the question that if secret agencies within the parameters of EU do not share intelligence on important matters, how would they cooperate within one agency?[1]

In 2015, there was a steady chain of publications and debates about intelligence sharing and security sector reforms in Europe, in which experts suggested major change to the present security and intelligence system that could not meet the requirements of counter terrorism operations. In several Eastern European states, the old infrastructure of security and intelligence mechanisms continues to inhibit the new security system in other member states.

Many states (Romania, Finland, Poland, Bosnia, Serbia and Bulgaria) introduced weak intelligence and security sector reforms that could not attract other states. After the Paris attacks, on December 18, 2015, the EU summit leader promised to improve intelligence sharing mechanism and coordination, but failed to persuade some states to extend their cooperation on the American war on terrorism. However, some states showed reservations and agreed to share intelligence only with those they trust because several European agencies feared that their secret information may well be in danger when so many partners are involved.[2]

The security system of the Belgian government faces numerous challenges to operate within the parameters of EU. Though the Netherlands' intelligence is competent, it needs even more improvements, while the French are working along modern lines to improve operational and counter terrorism capabilities of its intelligence agencies, which failed to intercept terrorists entering the country. The Belgian Foreign Minister warned that more intelligence on home-grown extremism is a must after the EU secret agencies came under heavy criticism immediately after they failed to share intelligence with France about the Paris attackers. French Interior Minister complained that no information about possible attacks was provided by EU secret agencies. French intelligence again failed to monitor the activities of its

---

[1] Ibid.
[2] Ibid.

home-growing extremists.

It is clear that the country's leaders are shying away from hard truths on the failure of their modern surveillance system. The issue of border checking is also in crisis as watch lists are maintained poorly, and the lack of up-to-date information further exacerbated in the problem. Guns and other firearms are still easily available in all EU states, which facilitate terrorists to carry out attacks on public places. In the UK, the presence of thousands of criminal gangs, dozens of terrorist networks, and the availability of arms raised serious questions. The way the government controls its population is violation of the right to privacy.

On February 11, 2016, the visiting professor of law in Queen Mary University London, Eric King criticized the UK government's new Investigatory Powers Bill and raw intelligence sharing mechanism: "Government's position is that the routine sharing of raw, unanalyzed intercepted materials is governed by "detailed internal guidance...and by a culture of compliance." But details behind the sharing taking place between friendly agencies are not visible in either statute, code of practice, public statement or policy." After the Paris attacks, there was a renewed push for a pan-European intelligence organization, but the Netherlands introduced its own security measures, and Britain and France renewed preventive measures to counter domestic extremist groups, while a common goal was missing.[1]

The Dutch state developed a strong surveillance program, which came under criticism from civil society and human rights organizations. The country intelligence reforms bill was submitted to parliament in September 2015, which granted security agencies far-reaching surveillance powers. Netherlands Institute of Human Rights warned that the bill violates privacy. However, the Netherlands' intelligence taps satellite data, but after the Snowden revelations, the government started spying on civilians. The country decided to share intelligence and data with other EU member states about jihadists fighting in Syria, Afghanistan, and Iraq.

In 2015, the Dutch Home Office was severely criticized after

---

[1] Ibid.

its revelations before parliament that more than 1.8 telecommunications intercepts had been collected by the NSA and gathered by the Dutch intelligence. In Sweden, intelligence operation is being led by National Defense Radio Establishment (NFRA), which is engaged in mass collection of data, but the country has not been able to counter radicalization on its soil. German intelligence agencies are looking at the US and UK through a hostile glass after the taping of Angela Merkel's personal telephone by NSA and UK's illegal surveillance operation in the country. In November 2015, in the EU meeting in Brussels, the issue of intelligence sharing was criticized by some states. "We have not overcome yet the hurdle of the exchange among intelligence services," Luxembourg's home minister told reporters. The crisis of mistrust in EU remains deep as Britain decided to leave the union if its reforms demands are not met. Their approach to counter terrorism is incoherent, contradictory and skeptical. The danger arising from the dismemberment of the union is real.[1]

---

[1] Ibid.

CHAPTER 3. THE EU CRISIS OF LAW ENFORCEMENT
COOPERATION

There is robust literature on the evolving perceptions of European Union (EU) intelligence cooperation to tackle the challenges of national security, and threats posed by home-grown extremist organizations. The basic information on the function and strategies of the intelligence agencies of the EU member states is not available to writers and researchers in order to analyze the factual security mechanism in the region, but some available information indicates that the EU intelligence sharing is in deep crisis. Since the EU secret agencies are handled by different formal and informal entities, researchers are unable to show the whole picture in a broad perspective.

When we read stories about the state and private intelligence agencies and their evolving function within the EU matrix, we come across numerous analyses and comments which point to the role of private agencies as a bigger challenge for the state agencies. The Paris terrorist attacks in 2015, followed by the Copenhagen and Brussels terror attacks in 2016, changed the whole picture of the professionalization of intelligence cooperation within the EU. Both state and private intelligence agencies failed to prevent the infiltration of terrorists into the countries.[1]

---

[1] *Daily Times*, 22 March 2016

The strategies EU have applied to counter radicalization and international terrorism suffered deep drawback after the Paris attacks. The failure of Belgium to eradicate or control radical groups and share intelligence information with the other states raised serious questions. Experts say the law enforcement agencies of the country are possibly divided on linguistic lines; therefore they could not deliver professionally. To restore the confidence of the people, the country needed to introduce security sector reforms and reorganization of its law enforcement infrastructure.

From Charlie Hebdo to the November 2015 terrorist attacks, the French intelligence has been under severe criticism for its inability to intercept or identify the attackers who killed dozens innocent civilians in Paris. The EU and Britain had long standing worries that the well-established networks of extremist and terrorist organizations in France can any time cause the environment of fear across the continent.[1]

Many relevant questions are being asked regarding the intelligence failure on the EU level that could not provide justified information about the terrorists' infiltration into France. Before these attacks, French intelligence (DGSE) and security services (DGSI) had identified the subversive intentions of the Islamic State (ISIS), Jabhat Al Nusrah and Paris-based extremist organizations, but no preventive measures were taken to secure the city. The increasing number of radicalized groups joining the ISIS ranks cause mistrust between the governments and civil society in the region. The Paris attacks diverted the attention of the EU member states to the issue of border management and control, to identify suspected terrorists and extremist elements crossing the continent. The Paris attackers were EU citizens who joined local extremist networks and trained within their secret camps.

While we look at the reluctant cooperation of the EU member states, and their flawed counter terrorism and counter intelligence strategies, we find more controversies in their national security approach. The political, legal and military establish-

[1] Ibid.

ment of the EU member states is deeply embroiled in political and sectarian conflicts, which pose serious threat to their security. When we discuss about their intelligence sharing on law enforcement level, only controversies, misperceptions, and unmentionable things swirls in our minds posing an unmanageable riddle. Their fear of each other's access to sensitive data and information of important state and private institutions is genuine, while the efforts of some strong and large state to impose their will on weak states are matter of great concern.[1]

In all the EU member states, thousands of asylum seekers from South Asia, Afghanistan and the Arab world showing fake identity documents (or none at all) claimed asylum, but their real identity is not known. Some have military training and financing for terrorist activities from their home states, and some receive financial support from their networks. EU citizens who became radicalized fighting in Syria, Iraq and Afghanistan returned with new ideologies, perceptions and resolves, but the lack of intelligence-sharing on these individuals received deep criticism from experts and print media. Britain presents the same tainted picture, where Muslim extremist and terrorist groups have established no-go areas across the country. On December 12, 2015, Daily Express reported the British police confirmed the existence of no-go areas in Britain where Muslim extremist and terrorist groups operate without fear. They are dancing in the streets and challenging the authority of the police.

Serving officers in terror-infected areas including London and Birmingham confirmed that their colleagues are dismal over the exacerbating threat of Islamic State-inspired attacks. Chief Inspector Police Wales and England, Sir Tom Winsor warned: "There are some communities born under other skies who will not involve the police at all...there are communities from other cultures who would prefer to police themselves." According to a Daily Mail report (January 18, 2014), in these areas rapes and murder cases are mostly going unreported and the rise of community justice is matter of great concern. "Parts of the UK are becoming no-go areas for police because minority communities

---

[1] Ibid.

are operating their own justice systems," the chief inspector of Constabulary warned.[1]

During the last two years, dozens intelligence and surveillance acts and laws were introduced by the Cameron government to improve the deteriorating law and order of the country, but most of these laws alienated citizens from the state. The recent violent wave of bomb blasts in Northern Ireland, targeted killing and the evolving nature of serious organized crime further exacerbated the pain of the British government. The UK intelligence and law enforcement agencies have been in deep pressure from terrorist networks across the country during the last three years. In a recent secret report by the authorities, it was revealed that the level of targeted killings in Britain reached the highest point.

Authorities are changing strategies, plans and mechanism time and again, but the result is nothing to show they are relevant. From the Home Office, and FCO to the recently established Security Innovation and Demonstration Centre (SIDC) and the police, all institutions are struggling to maintain law and order in the country, but their flawed enforcement strategies, weak security approach, wrongly designed surveillance strategies, and watchdogs failed to deliver or positively respond to the prevailing violent criminal culture across the country. In fact, powerful intelligence agencies of the country are playing on opposite directions. The EU intelligence analysis centre, intelligence division of the EU military staff, signal intelligence analysis, Europol, EU counter terrorism group, the EU border management agency, and the EU satellite centre have also failed to provide reliable intelligence information to the policy makers. Researcher Janani Krishnaswamy describes the causes of intelligence failure:

> The literature review on the state of intelligence theorizing in the West has clearly documented the sharp differences among the various theoretical traditions of

---

[1]According to a *Daily Mail* report (January 18, 2014), in these areas rapes and murder cases are mostly going unreported and the rise of community justice is matter of great concern.

intelligence studies. While a majority of the Western theoretical discourses have focused on intelligence failures, each of them has approached intelligence failures differently and has consequently provided direction for intelligence reforms in relation to the hypothesized causes. Yet, no theory can be all encompassing and address all failures of the intelligence community. However, the root cause of the various failures of the intelligence community in India predominantly exists in the failure to sufficiently understand such causes. It is essential to create a theory to: (a) help intelligence review committees analyze intelligence failures with more clarity and rigor, (b) facilitate them — inquiry committees and policy makers — in determining which failures of the intelligence community are more urgent and (c) systematize the intelligence reform making process.[1]

In his recent research paper, Camino Mortera argued that the EU is responsible for harmonizing counter-terrorism measures in national criminal systems. The framework decision on combating terrorism, adopted in 2002, requires member-states to introduce in their criminal codes provisions penalizing terrorism and harmonizing punishments for terrorist offences.[2]

One of the main characteristics of attacks since the Mohamed Merah case in March 2012 is that the perpetrators were all "well known" to the intelligence services. And in France, some were the subject of a special file kept when a person is considered to be a threat to the security of the state. Some 6,000 Europeans are involved in the fighting in Syria. If EU has 6,000 "active" jihadists, that probably means that if we try to count those who were not identified, the logistics people who help them join up, their sympathizers and the most radical extremists who are not yet involved in violence but are on the verge of it.[3]

---

[1] Janani Krishnaswamy. "Why Intelligence Fails," *Policy Report* No. 3, 2013, The Hindu Centre for Politics and Public Policy, cited in *The Telegraph*, 22 March 2016.
[2] Ibid.
[3] Ibid.

One of the challenges facing French intelligence is tracking the movement of hundreds of French radicals passing over Turkey's border with northern Syria, Islamic State's stronghold, and identifying significant threats. French investigators are concerned they may have overlooked a clue supplied by Turkey in December 2014: Two Frenchmen, Omar Mostefai and Samy Amimour, had crossed together into Syria with a third person a little more than a year earlier, said Turkish officials and other people familiar with the matter.[1]

[1] *Wall Street Journal,* Paris Attacks Show Cracks in France's Counterterrorism Effort, by David Gautheirs, 23 Nov 2015.

CHAPTER 4. THE EUROPEAN UNION STARTS TO KEEL OVER: INTELLIGENCE AGENCIES AND THE CRISIS OF INTELLIGENCE SHARING

The European Union is mired in a deep security and financial crisis. The crisis is going to worsen as tensions among member states pick up. The EU's struggles to bring stability to central and South Eastern European regions can be seen in the context of the complexity of its internal crisis, where former Soviet bloc states do not welcome the U.S.-backed international security agenda, and do not want to follow Americanized way of intelligence information collection and surveillance mechanism against their own citizens. The crisis of financial insecurity is still lingering. Poor and weak states are angry over the attitude of the rich and powerful states who want to dominate the process of political and economic policy making.[1]

The turmoil at the Eastern EU border, particularly in Moldova and Greece, continues to exacerbate. Amid this deepening crisis, the EU lacks a professional strategic outlook to keep the project together. The idea that all states should work for a common objective failed due to the lack of a common security policy. Europe's major internal security threat and the fear of Russian aggression together with the refugee crisis will continue to cause problems.

---

[1] *Daily Times*, March 01, 2016.

On December 3, 2015, Denmark refused to go ahead with the bloc integration movement and the joining of policies associated with freedom, security and justice in the EU. The reluctance of member states to cooperate on law enforcement and intelligence sharing shows that they want to retain their national sovereignty on these issues and they want to improve the performance of the weak and staggering union.[1]

Intelligence sharing and cooperation in the field of law enforcement has often been mentioned as the heart of counterterrorism efforts within the EU, but we still wait for a smart reforms package that could address all outstanding issues. The fundamental benefit of intelligence sharing is to build confidence among states, but the case of EU states is different and disappointing due to the lack of trust and confidence-building measures. They look at each other through different glasses, making murky the intelligence sharing picture.

We understand that every intelligence agency of member states is competent and has its own cultural and geographical approach towards national and international security, but at the EU level, they are conservative and reluctant to share their country's information with another state. This complicated way of partnership is the fundamental obstruction in bringing them to the point of common interest. The case is further complicated as all EU states' intelligence agencies are not fully interdependent on each other in the field of counterterrorism and counterintelligence.

Though The Hague Programme introduced guidance and principles of law enforcement information exchange, even that failed to convince member states to cooperate with each other. However, the Stockholm Programme (2010–2015), which laid the foundation of a coherent and consolidated law enforcement cooperation approach, remained ineffective in helping to improve confidence-building measures among member states. The Schengen Information System (SIS) is the only information exchange system sharing body, but it is only valid within the EU. The SIS was upgraded in 2015 to ensure the availability of information regarding any terrorist threat.[2]

---

[1] Ibid.
[2] Ibid.

Edward Snowden's revelations about the secret cooperation of some member states with the United States' National Security Agency (NSA) in spying on other states caused further mistrust. In 2015, it was revealed that German intelligence spied on the EU British foreign policy chief and tried to tap the mobile phone of U.S. Secretary of State John Kerry. After these revelations, the EU member states redeemed the establishment of multilateral venues for intelligence sharing and an independent EU intelligence agency to coordinate their efforts in tackling radicalization and terrorism across the continent. In November 2015, the Paris attacks brought renewed focus on the establishment of a common intelligence agency, because the intelligence failure in France and Sweden showed that intelligence information sharing has been in trouble since the Madrid and London attacks.[1]

Before the Paris attacks, there were plans to enhance security cooperation among EU members, but the changing nature of their priorities and reluctance to understand each other diminished all hopes. National interests and sovereignty are the fundamental hurdles that discourage member states from sharing important information at the Union level, but the lack of trust among intelligence agencies is a matter of serious concern. Among the agencies, the difference in organizational structures is also an irksome challenge. It is a very difficult task to streamline or materialize intelligence cooperation among member states due to the problem, which derives from the nature of national intelligence agencies and the absence of an effective institutionalizing mechanism.

The most important thing is that the EU intelligence agencies could not priorities the threat, and did not realize the importance of a common intelligence platform to streamline the flow of information from one state to another. Some states like Kosovo, Greece, Sweden, and Netherlands are embroiled in the fight against radicalization and extremism within their borders; therefore, they have shown some reservations that other member states do not take interest in helping them defeat this hydra. Consequently, the unity of the EU is under serious threat. In fact, the present EU has become more difficult to run than the

---

[1] *US Today*, 22 March 2016.

EU of 1989. The inclusion of former Communist states into the Union caused a ripple. The conflagration between some states over their control of the EU could shake the foundation of political integration as Britain is set to exit. If things are not settled, the keel over of the EU could be the biggest geopolitical event of 2016.[1]

The Netherlands fights radicalization and extremism

The war in Iraq and Afghanistan caused many disastrous incidents in Europe and South Asia. As we discussed in previous chapters, EU is facing the crisis of information and intelligence sharing. All member states have their own problems and their own ways of gathering information to protect their citizens. As competent and professional as the Netherlands intelligence infrastructure may be, the networks of extremist organizations and ISIS challenge the authority of the state. Professor Arun Kundnani (2015) has also pointed to the same issue in the European Union member states in his research paper:

> The disastrous consequences of the Iraq war soon became apparent by 2005, counter terrorism policy makers were looking for new models that could help them understand not just 9/11 but also how to prevent bombings carried out by European citizens, such as those that took place in Madrid in 2004 and London in 2005. At this point, the concept of radicalization became central to the emerging analysis of the causes of terrorism in national security circles.[2]

While we look at the changing picture of intelligence and policing priorities in the Netherlands, it appears that the country has become embroiled in a deep security crisis as its war on radicalization is causing the social and political alienation of minorities. Like in Romania, Poland, Malaysia, India and Pakistan, intelligence and security sector reforms received little attention from the successive governments in the past. With the changing

[1] *Daily Times*, March 01, 2016.
[2] Professor Arun Kundnani (2015) has also pointed to the same issue in the European Union member states in his research paper, "A Decade Lost: Rethinking Radicalization and Extremism," 2015.

intelligence and security picture in Europe, the development, coordination and articulation of national security policies of countries have become critically important.

The Dutch police system has been under pressure from communities and outlaw elements since the 2000s, therefore, critical debates have often pointed towards the need for deep reforms. Insecurity and administrative problems for the Dutch police are too irksome. The recent police reforms in the country are characterized by one-sided centralization of policing policy, while the local dimension has been left out of reforms. From outside the Netherlands policing reforms look strong with a professional arrangement, but if we look inside the organization, it is quite weak. Moreover, the Netherlands' Country Police Act does not provide much information about local policing or what kind of policing the country needs.

After the Cold War era, the Netherlands' national security apparatus was reorganized. Many law enforcement and security policies were established to tackle the menace of political Islam and emerging cyber security threats, but these policies proved ineffective in intercepting Arab extremists, dancing in the streets of Amsterdam, The Hague and Rotterdam from 2004 to 2015. With this evolving nature of national security threats, the principles of traditional law enforcement and intelligence information gathering also changed. After 9/11 and the emergence of political Islam in the Netherlands, extremism and radicalization further transformed the culture of law enforcement and the intelligence mechanism. The recent killings in France left diverse impact on social stratification while the trend of racism rose again and discrimination took root in mainstream society with uncontrollable speed.

On November 27, 2015, the government submitted four bills to parliament on the integrated approach to tackling jihadism, combating violent groups and managing the prevailing radicalization in the country. The plan contained strong preventive measures important for law enforcement authorities, which set the countering terrorism strategy as a first priority. Under the second bill: "The passport and identity of anyone who is subject to a travel ban imposed by the minister of security and justice will be cancelled automatically with immediate effect." This bill is not so different from the travel ban in the UK. This means to prevent jihadists from travelling to Afghanistan, Syria, Iraq, Pakistan, Yemen and other violence affected states.[1]

As the country faces the threat of cyber terrorism, another bill was also introduced in parliament to counter financial and economic terrorism with an effective cyber security strategy. In 2011, the Netherlands' government published its first cyber security strategy to counter the prevailing culture of hacking important data from state institutions. In 2013, the strategy was reviewed and published to easily identify cyber terrorists and professional criminals. Digital fraud and theft of information became common while financial terrorism continued to target banks and local industry. As digital espionage remained a violent threat in the country, on November 17, 2015, the government published an updated version of its Cyber Security Assessment. However, in view of the exacerbating threat of cyber terrorism and hacking in the country, the government also submitted the first cyber security bill to the house of parliament.[2]

In the Netherlands, jihadism has spread across the country into a complex and dynamic movement, which poses a precarious challenge to the national security of the country. A recent report on the Dutch intelligence agency (AIVD) is a stern warning to the law enforcement authorities and to the government in power that terrorist networks pose serious security threats. Wars in Afghanistan, Syria and Yemen provoked violent forces in the country. Home-grown extremism has also forced the government and law enforcement agencies to introduce laws and reorganize preventive measures.

During a protest rally against Islamization in the Netherlands on November 9, 2015, police seized a cartoon of Prophet

---

[1] On November 27, 2015, the government submitted four bills to parliament on the integrated approach towards tackle jihadism, combating violent groups and managing the prevailing radicalization in the country.

[2] November 17, 2015, the government published an updated version of its Cyber Security Assessment. However, in view of the exacerbating threat of cyber terrorism and hacking in the country, the government also submitted the first cyber security bill to the house of parliament. *Daily Times*, 02 February 2016

Muhammad (PBUH) that was offensive to Muslims. Dutch news reported the arrest of 32 protestors. However, Militant Islam Monitor also reported the defection of a Dutch Air Force sergeant, a 26-year-old Moroccan-Dutch, to Islamic State (IS) in Syria. According to a Dutch newspaper (De Telegram), the sergeant had access to secret information. Police across the country then kept 350 extremist Muslims (of which 130 live in The Hague) under secret surveillance. The involvement of a growing number of Dutch jihadists participating in the conflicts in the Middle East and Persian Gulf regions is a blemish on the state's security agencies. Police and intelligence agencies have so far failed to prevent jihadists from going to war zones in Syria, Iraq and Yemen.[1]

Though the government claims that 38 measures within the Integrated Approach to Jihadism Action Programme are the answer to jihadist threat, in a true sense, many things are not going in the right direction as the police have failed to closely monitor sleeper cells across the country. In 2013, the Interior Ministry confiscated 150 passports of those who had intended to leave the country for jihad and more than 90 social benefits paid to jihadists were cancelled but no improvement occurred in addressing this issue.

This way of addressing jihadism has been severely criticized in intellectual circles and by local media. The ISIS network is spreading across the country uncontrollably even as the government has entered an unending war with it. "IS is our enemy and that is why we are at war," the Dutch Prime Minister said. The Minister of Security and Justice concurred, saying that the threat of a terror attack was real. Threats to the security of the Netherlands are constantly changing and are becoming increasingly intertwined. Though Dutch intelligence is competent in countering radicalization in the country, a clear picture of preventive measures is still bleak.[2]

In response to the report that one of the perpetrators of the Brussels attacks had been expelled to the Netherlands, the Min-

---

[1] Ibid.
[2] The Minister of Security and Justice commented on October 5, 2015, on the occasion of updating the 38th edition of the Terrorist Threat Assessment.

ister of Security and Justice wrote the following letter to the House of Representatives.[1]

> The Permanent Parliamentary Committee on Security and Justice asked me on 24 March 2016 to respond to the report that one of the perpetrators of the Brussels attacks was expelled to the Netherlands. The Minister of Foreign Affairs joins me in providing the requested information. First, I will respond to the questions asked. If the attacker was expelled to the Netherlands by Turkey, on what grounds was that done? The Turkish authorities asked Ibrahim El Bakraoui to leave the country and then facilitated a flight from Istanbul to Amsterdam on 14 July 2015. The grounds on which this was done were not known to the Dutch authorities:

> 1. Was there a link to the Netherlands?

> *There was no link to the Netherlands known to us.*

> 2. Was he suspected of any criminal offences at that time? If so, in what country or countries was this known? Was he detained in the Netherlands?

> *No suspicions against him were known in the Netherlands. He was not registered in the relevant investigation databases. He was not detained in the Netherlands.*

> 3. Was the Netherlands involved in the investigation to determine whether he had a criminal record, this in the light of the suggestion that Belgium was faced with a lack of evidence?

> *The Netherlands was not involved in this investigation into a possible criminal record.*

> The Minister of Security and Justice went on to present further information on the situation.

---

[1] 24 March 2016. https://www.government.nl/documents/parliamentary-documents/2016/03/24/letter-to-parliament-in-response-to-the-report-that-one-of-the-perpetrators-of-the-brussels-attacks-was-expelled-to-the-netherlands.

General Counterterrorism Measures in the Netherlands

Since the 9/11 attacks in 2001, the government has taken a series of general measures to combat terrorism. For example:

1. Websites that use hate speech or call for violence or discrimination are taken down.

2. The Counterterrorism Alert System warns the government and key sectors (drinking water companies, the energy sector) about terrorist threats.

3. The Royal Netherlands Air Force monitors Dutch airspace around the clock.

4. Special units from the armed forces and the police collaborate in the Special Intervention Service (DSI). This service arrests and detains those suspected of terrorist offences. In the most extreme cases it eliminates them.

5. The police monitor people who may pose a terrorist threat.

6. European countries work closely with each other to combat terrorism. For example, the European Union has a Counter-Terrorism Coordinator who harmonizes the counterterrorism activities of the member states.

7. The government has taken measures to combat terrorist financing.

8. The intelligence and security services have increased their capabilities.

Chapter 5. The Reluctant Partnership of Eastern European States: Russian and US Strategies

Media assertions that the Russian civilian and military intelligence are stepping up their influence in Eastern and Western Europe have raised many questions. There is speculation that the Russian government and its intelligence agencies are promoting an anti-West propaganda campaign while offering economic packages to weak states. New Eastern Europe Magazine (linked to Radio Free Europe and other Western agencies) has warned of an exponentially growing influence of President Putin in Eastern Europe: "From France to Greece to Hungary, he is cultivating parties of Europe's far right and left; anyone who might lobby for Russian interests in the EU, or even help to prize the union apart."

The case of Russian influence in Eastern Europe is complicated. Central and Eastern European/South Eastern European (CEE/SEE) countries, formerly close allies of Russia, are now a major trading and financial partner for the euro zone. The annual surplus in the balance of payments with euro zone countries is estimated at €60 billion. The overall growth rate in Eastern European countries is expected to be positive in 2016, but Hungary and the Baltic states are likely to face recession. The United States still faces tough opposition in the continent. Russian influence is expanding and some say it is funding political parties to oppose to the military buildup of the United States and NATO in the region, including the Baltic States.

In March 2014, on the heels of the violent Western-backed coup that removed the elected leader of Ukraine, the Crimean Peninsula left Ukraine and rejoined the Russia Federation. This move seems to have been supported by the majority of the population of Crimea, who voted in a referendum, but it was opposed by the majority of citizens of the rest of Ukraine (although simultaneously, two eastern Ukraine provinces also sought to secede). Unbiased numbers regarding popular opinion may not be available, but the strategic importance of Crimea cannot be over emphasized. It is home to Russia's only warm-water submarine base. Losing that asset, and having the location taken over by a hostile force, would obviously have been devastating to Russia's national security. At the same time, the New York Times reported on the White House plan to buy billions of dollars worth of weapons for Europe, despite matters having been "quieted" in Eastern Ukraine:

> The White House plans to pay for the additional weapons and equipment with a budget request of more than $3.4 billion for military spending in Europe in 2017, several officials said Monday, more than quadrupling the current budget of $789 million. The weapons and equipment will be used by American and NATO forces, ensuring that the alliance can maintain a full armored combat brigade in the region at all times. Though Russia's military activity has quieted in eastern Ukraine in recent months, Moscow continues to maintain a presence there, working with pro-Russian local forces. Administration officials said the additional NATO forces were calculated to send a signal to President Vladimir V. Putin that the West remained deeply suspicious of his motives in the region.[1]

Ukraine's new president Petro Poroshenko told the European Commission that President Vladimir Putin had privately

---

[1] "U.S. Fortifying Europe's East to Deter Putin," Mark Landler and Helene Cooper, *The New York Times*, 01 February 2016.

noted that he could have invaded Poland, Romania and the Baltic states any time, if that had been his intention.

"If I wanted, in two days I could have Russian troops not only in Kiev, but also in Riga, Vilnius, Tallinn, Warsaw and Bucharest," Mr. Putin is said to have told President Petro Poroshenko of Ukraine. Mr. Putin's alleged threat bears similarities to remarks he made to Jose Manuel Barroso, the president of the European Commission: "If I want to, I can take Kiev in two weeks."[1] The Russian President made these comments in a series of telephone conversations with Mr. Poroshenko over the current ceasefire in eastern Ukraine. Mr. Putin also warned Mr. Poroshenko not to put too much faith in the EU, saying that Russia could exert its influence and bring about a "blocking minority" among member states. The EU recently announced further sanctions against Russia, focusing on the energy, financial and arms sectors. But there have been divisions among member states over sanctions, with many complaining that their own economies are suffering.

The US claims to be particularly nervous about Russian intentions in the Baltic States, and Mr. Obama sought to reassure them with his speech in Tallinn earlier in 2016. Any threat to send Russian troops into the capitals of Latvia, Lithuania, Estonia, Poland and Romania would cause grave alarm.

President Putin and his allies in the region have vowed to respond "asymmetrically" to the major US military buildup in Europe. On 31 March 2016, RT (Russian Television) reported that the Russian envoy to NATO had reiterated Russian resolve to resist the inclusion of Ukraine and Georgia in NATO: "We are not passive observers, we consistently take all the military measures we consider necessary in order to counter balance this reinforced presence that is not justified by anything," Aleksandr Grushko said.

The United States also accused Russia of secretly funding political parties in EU member states. Moreover, Daily Telegraph reported US intelligence had conducted a major investigation into how the Kremlin was infiltrating political parties in Europe. James Clapper, the U.S. head of national intelligence, was

---

[1] *The Telegraph*, 02 Sept. 2014.

instructed by Congress to conduct a major review of clandestine Russian funding of European parties over the past decade. The review reflects mounting concerns in Washington over Moscow's determination to exploit European disunity in order to undermine the NATO bloc's US missile defense programs and revoke the punitive economic sanctions regime imposed on Russia after the "annexation" of Crimea.

European newspapers have warned that Russian intelligence is actively expanding its influence in Eastern Europe where several states want to join the EU. They report that Mr. Putin is seeking to change the attitude of the political leaders of Bosnia, Serbia, Georgia, Ukraine and Moldova. Moscow has re-established some influence in Hungary, in part through a package of financial assistance to help Hungary in maintaining major gas and nuclear projects. In Budapest, the prime minister of the country strongly opposed EU sanctions against Russia, while the Slovak leader, Robert Fico, also criticized the EU for its action against Moscow.

In a widely reported speech in July 2014, Mr. Orban "denounced the West European democratic model as an obsolete failure and held up Putin as a template for a modern successful leader. In January he met Putin in Moscow secretly, secured a 10bn line of credit from the Russians, and awarded contracts to Moscow building of two new reactors at Hungary's sole nuclear power plant."[1]

Russia's Federal Security Services also devoted considerable attention to recruiting Baltic businessmen, politicians and former members of their ranks. Russian intelligence penetration of these states is high, as is its media influence. And it dominates the supply of energy and electricity to the Baltic States, and has not hesitated to use that leverage to influence these nations. Furthermore, Russia's conventional and nuclear deployments cover the entire Baltic Sea area. From its fortified base at Kaliningrad, Russia can project power not only into the Baltic Sea but also to Poland and Germany.

Even in the Netherlands, claims have been made of Russian influence, this time on a referendum over whether to block the

---

[1] *Guardian*, 29 October 2014.

EU's closer relations with Ukraine. UK sources said the arguments deployed in support of the referendum "closely resembled" known Russian propaganda. Senior British government officials told The Sunday Telegraph of growing fears that "a new Cold War" was now unfolding in Europe, with Russian meddling taking on a breadth, range and depth far greater than previously thought.

Seeking to counter Russian influence, the United States decided to deploy more forces in Eastern Europe. In 2016, the US budget for the program stood at $789.3 million. For the next year, President Obama asked for some $3.4 billion. To Russia and to some Western European countries, this figure seems excessive, while Eastern European NATO members ask for more. The truth lies in the middle. The U.S. European Command (EUCOM) and the U.S. Africa Command (AFRICOM) share many facilities, forces, and assets. In response to Eastern European concerns, U.S. reassurances have implied some re-deployments—some of which periodical—of assets already present in the European theatre. Troops and aircraft from bases in Italy, Germany, and the United Kingdom have been sent to Bulgaria, Estonia, Hungary, and Poland.

Central Asian states that were formerly part of the USSR are also in play. The difference between Central Asia and Ukraine is that Ukraine borders on the European Union. For the countries of Central Asia, there will be no European Economic Framework Agreement and there is no prospect of future NATO membership. Under severe American pressure, in 2001, Kyrgyzstan leased an airport to the United States for use by NATO forces in Afghanistan. In 2014, the lease was allowed to expire.

Chapter 6. The Crisis of Britain's Law Enforcement, Intelligence and Surveillance Mechanism

Law is enforced in social and cultural ways to protect citizens, national critical infrastructure, and to prevent crimes, terror attacks, violence and extremism. As law enforcement is a societal function necessary for internal stability, society exercises a form of social control of behavior through the process of law enforcement. In the UK, the law is enforced through CCTV cameras fitted in every corner of buildings, roads, houses, buses, trains, toilets, schools, colleges, traffic lights and even within street lights. Despite all these precautions, crime and terror related incidents continue to increase. The UK strongest surveillance system (TEMPORA), helicopters, drones and other means of intelligence are in the skies recording conversations and scanning houses and offices to protect us from criminal gangs and terrorist attacks but, unfortunately, all these security measures have failed to address the complaints of the business and investment communities. The London police commissioner recently warned that law enforcement agencies had lost the trust of communities after the revelations of Edward Snowden.[1]

---

[1] *Law Enforcement in the United States*, James A. Conser, Rebecca Paynich, Terry Gingerich, Terry E. Gingerich, Jones & Bartlett Publishers, 21 Oct 2011

Mr. Otto von Bismarck once said, "Only a fool learns from his own mistakes; the wise man learns from the mistakes of others." The way we tackle security issues caused many negative perceptions and social discontent in our society. Research reports of London-based think tanks raised important questions about the performance of state institutions and their mode of operation. Corruption, racism and discrimination have left an ugly blot on the UK's multicultural face, and Scotland Yard and the Home Office are in hot water as their forces have failed to demonstrate their professionalism. After every six months, the government announces new security and immigration measures, indicative of its frustration and anxiety to control the prevailing environment of fear and discontent. However, we have lost our destiny and are now looking for a light to come out of this social quagmire.[1]

According to an English proverb, there is a solution for everything even though there are doubts. The police and its private partners are failing to intercept and investigate serious organized crime and sexual abuse cases properly. According to the recently released Police Watchdog report, the police is stuck in the past, using outdated methods to deal with modern, organized criminal networks across the country. Notwithstanding their access to modern technology, which enables them to act professionally, police officers lack proper skills, training and education? In the Rotherham child abuse case, the police chief admitted failure:

> This is a hideous crime. I am deeply embarrassed. I can say with honesty I had no idea of the scale and scope of this." However, the Home Affairs Select Committee also criticized the former chief constable on how his ignorance over these activities was "totally unconvincing."[2]

In February 2015, The Independent reported the failure of Essex police to investigate 30 child abuse claims. Vulnerable children were left at the mercy of a child sex offender after a police unit delayed the arrests of suspects during more than three

[1] *Daily Times*, 07 April, 2015
[2] Ibid.

years of systemic failure, the newspaper reported. Later on, the chief constable of the Essex police apologized. On November 27, 2014, Her Majesty's Inspectorate of Constabulary (HMIC) published a report that criticized the police force for its inability to demonstrate its professionalism.

On March 9, 2015, BBC reported that Dal Babu, a former Chief Superintendent of London police, said that many Muslims did not trust the prevent strategy. The police approach to law enforcement is quite peculiar, which typically involves waiting until a crime has been committed and then attempting to tackle it and arrest the criminal through flawed arrest strategies. This kind of approach no longer works as professional criminal gangs from Asia and Europe have adopted new strategies and technologies. The performance of the National Crime Agency (NCA) is also in question as the parameters of drug trafficking, serious organized crime, human trafficking and fake currency trade have expanded.[1]

Corruption in our state institutions is a matter of great concern. This disease deeply affects the performance of government. The threat of institutional corruption still needs to be recognized. In the National Security Strategy (NSS) of 2010, the word corruption has been mentioned only on page 13. However, the Strategic Defense and Security Review (SDSR) 2010, which fleshes out some aspects and the NSS's implementation strategies, do not mention corruption at all. This inconsistent behavior in the UK's policymaking process indicates that corruption is not yet seen as relevant to all aspects of national security. This is a serious mistake that directly affects the development of an integrated strategy for reducing the risk of looming security threats.[2]

Hate crimes, motivated jihadism, targeted killing, and the scourge of Islam-phobia have significantly intensified in London. Faith-related attacks have increased and Muslim students

---

[1] On March 9, 2015, *BBC* reported that Dal Babu, a former chief superintendent London police, said that many Muslims did not trust the prevention strategy. The police approach to law enforcement is quite peculiar, which typically involves waiting until a crime has been committed and then attempting to tackle it and arrest the criminal.

[2] The 2015 UK National Security Strategy, *Briefing Paper Number 7431, 14* December 2015, Jon Lunn and Eleanor Scarnell.

are suffering backlash and abuse in schools. Recently, The Independent reported that a teenage Muslim student at a school in Oxfordshire was slapped and called a "terrorist." Members of the teachers union told the newspaper that there was an increase in Islamophobic incidents with the 400,000 Muslim students in schools increasingly likely to be jeered at as "terrorists," "pedophiles" or "immigrants." However, anti-Semitic incidents too reached a high level with record damage to property, abuse and threats. A Jewish NGO recorded more than 1,168 incidents in 2014. The home secretary termed the figure "deeply concerning." Criminal money continues to be channeled through UK banks to terrorists.[1]

Every day, the threat of terrorism and violent extremism is growing, which makes the police overactive. Racism has affected the law enforcement efforts of the police. Racial inequality in the workplace has also worsened. The Macpherson Enquiry Report asserted that institutional racism brought a bad name to the UK. There are some pieces of legislation that remain ineffective. The government has placed terrorism as the top threat to the country but the response to it has been unsatisfactory. The Prime Minister has shown little or no interest in foreign policy and national security issues. The police need to improve their performance and reduce costs. Our policing must evolve along with the social make up of communities, inequalities and divisions. We need to create a police force that is professional, and accountable.[2]

National Crime Agency and Cyber Crime

As we critically discussed the performance of the National Crime Agency (NCA), the details of the agency functions are mostly comprised on its website elucidation, so I decided to include a brief profile of that important institution in this book. There are several unites operating within the matrix of NCA, therefore, we need to highlight specific units. One is the National Crime Cyber Unit (NCCU), which leads the UK's response to cyber crime, supports partners with specialist capabilities and

---

[1] *The Independent*, 23 January 2015
[2] *Carnegie Europe*, 18 February 2015

coordinates the national response to the most serious of cyber crime threats. Working closely with the Regional Organized Crime Units (ROCUs), the MPCCU (Metropolitan Police Cyber Crime Unit), partners within Industry, Government and International Law Enforcement, the NCCU has the capability to respond rapidly to changing threats.

Using the NCA's single intelligence picture, the NCCU works with partners to identify and understand the growing use of cyber as an enabler across all crime types. It can then determine the most effective ways of tackling the threat. The NCCU is a recipient of funding from the National Cyber Security Program, which supports development and transformation of the UK's cyber capabilities across Government. The NCCU has strong links with the ROCUs and local Police Services, sharing information, intelligence and expertise to enhance knowledge of the cyber threat in order to priorities operational and disruption activity most effectively. The NCCU, ROCUs and local Police forces routinely conduct operations in partnership.

The UK's controversial approach towards national security

In the UK society, there are several ways to view the recent evolution. Some sociologists look through scientific lenses while others take an intellectual approach in perceiving the dynamics of social transformation. When one talks about security and terrorism in the UK, he comes across many ideas, hypotheses and reports about the government and its agencies' failure in tackling violent extremism and international terrorism. There are thousands of research papers, essays, speeches and lectures available on the websites of think tanks, newspapers, journals and libraries that address the crisis of national security with different approaches, but the lack of professional approach and coordination in these research materials makes the case worse.

In this chapter, my main focus will be on the weak approach of the UK government towards law enforcement and its counter terrorism mechanism. However, some aspects of controversial intelligence and surveillance mechanism will also be elucidated. As we have already experienced the introduction of new surveillance technologies and their controversial use in our society, these weapons have badly failed to intercept jihadists joining the ranks of the Islamic State of Iraq and Syria (ISIS) and other groups in the Middle East and South Asia.[1]

We also understand that with the introduction of modern communication systems, surveillance and espionage networks have become a global phenomenon. The capturing, tracing and processing of the personal data of citizens have become a controversial issue worldwide. Every state has promulgated its own communication and surveillance law that allows interception of communication; stops e-mail trafficking and monitor Facebook, Twitter and YouTube. While we discuss these law enforcement related issues, many new things come to mind that raise the question of whether surveillance is truly the only solution to our social problems. The focus of the intelligence agencies on international terrorism, and specific ethnic communities within the country, cause great concern and alienates the citizens from the state. Yes, we know that modern state machinery in the UK ultimately depends on surveillance data but the way surveillance is used against the privacy of citizens has prompted deep frustration and social alienation.

The UK's citizens are well aware of their privacy rights protected by international law, but the law in the UK takes a weak and fractured approach towards privacy. Communities complain that the current legal and regulatory system is not providing adequate protection for personal information. At present, in the UK, the multi-faceted surveillance strategy has become flawed and needs to be reformed to ensure that the right of privacy in the European Convention on Human Rights is honored. Article eight of the European Convention on Human Rights provides everyone with the right of respect for his private and family life, his home and his correspondence, and that there shall be no interference by a public authority with the exercise of this right except such as is in accordance with the law. In our society, in the presence of the Interception Communication Law and Regulation of Investigatory Power Act 2000 (RIPA), and TEM-

---

[1] *National Cyber Crime Unit*, http://www.nationalcrimeagency.gov. uk/about-us/what-we-do/national-cyber-crime-unit. *Daily Times*, 18 November 2014

PORA, privacy has become a joke while the Data Protection Act and RIPA have never explained to the citizens what happens to their personal information.

This approach is very weak and the trust between the state's security apparatus, law enforcement agencies and the citizens has been undermined. On November 6, 2014, The Guardian reported that Sir Bernard Hogan-Howe, Commissioner of the Metropolitan police in London, told a conference of senior police chiefs that law enforcement agencies in the UK had lost the public's trust after the disclosures on government surveillance made by Mr. Edward Snowden. "We need to ensure that where law enforcement accesses private communications there is a process of authorization, oversight and governance that gets the balance right between the individual's right to privacy and their right to be protected from serious crime," said the police chief. But the issue is quite different as the police are not fully cooperating with communities.[1]

The government and its agencies are deeply frustrated due to the looming security crisis and widening sphere of extremism and foreign espionage around us. The intelligence war is another quagmire we have been trapped in. Our agencies are fighting in different directions against this abruptly imposed war. We know the UK intelligence gained professional experience in countering terrorism and foreign espionage during the last 100 years, but this time they face the most professionally trained and technologically adorned networks. The increasing number of dangers transcending national boundaries is reflected in the government's weak approach to law enforcement and counter-terrorism. An evolving Asian, African and European intelligence policy towards the UK raises several questions, including the recent attitude of France, China, Russia and Germany. Germany cancelled a Cold War era pact with the UK in response to the revelations of Mr. Snowden about TEMPORA's electronic surveillance operations.

---

[1] On November 6, 2014, *The Guardian* reported that Sir Bernard Hogan-Howe, commissioner of the Metropolitan police in London, told a conference of senior US police chiefs that law enforcement agencies in the UK had lost the public's trust after the disclosures on government surveillance made by Mr. Edward Snowden.

September 01, 2014, David Cameron said that his government was considering introducing some national security measures. These included confiscating the passports of UK extremists, excluding them from the country and placing them on no-fly list arrangements on a statutory footing but the Prime Minister could not implement these security measures. Social scientists and independent experts confirm that the UK's counterterrorism strategy is failing to tackle the danger of violent extremism and international terrorism. These experts attribute this failure to the controversial approach to counterterrorism and domestic extremism strategy. As the national security environment for the UK has changed, the country perceives its national security threat emanates from the terrorist and jihadist groups of the Middle East and South Asia.[1]

The arrival of hundreds of criminal gangs and serious organized networks from Asia, Africa and European Union states has caused deep frustration and vulnerability in the government and private sectors. Business communities are under threat from these criminal mafia groups that use modern technologies in smashing the doors of offices, shops and houses. The arrival of these illiterate and unskilled individuals has forced the government to introduce new laws, new restrictions, new internet and privacy strategies, new watchdog programs and online policing. To tackle all the above-mentioned threats, the government and its agencies need to adopt policies based on the principles of the local culture. We need laws based on our culture and social principles. We do not need to follow the US or European way of countering terrorism. We need to stick to our cultural and social way of countering radicalization; we don't need to follow the US designed counterterrorism strategies.

Notwithstanding Whitehall's very robust commitment towards protecting UK citizens from any abrupt terrorist attack, public confidence, trust and satisfaction between the police and communities have steadily declined. The Prime Minister allocated about 130 million pounds for MI5 to help identify lone wolves, and vowed to give more power to MI5 and MI6 for tackling domestic and international terrorism. In the new counter-

---

[1] *Daily Times*, 18 November 2014.

terrorism and security bill, some measures have also been added including the countering of radicalization and powers to stop people heading abroad to join the Islamic State (IS) networks.

The coverage regarding the failure of our way of policing printed in newspapers and electronic media is typically perceived as more credible than the braying of our politicians and Ministers. The list of threats and security gaps are endless, ranging from lone wolves returning from the Middle East and South Asia to the trends of jihadism across the country. Recently, parliament's intelligence and security committee inquiry into how terrorists killed a UK soldier in East London, termed it as an intelligence failure. The inquiry also warned that the existing government strategies that aim to undermine extremism were not working as 1,000 radicalized Muslims had reached Iraq and Syria for jihad.

As extremist and jihadist forces have encircled us from all sides, we remain in the middle; neither can we go back nor can we proceed to our destination. On November 26, 2014, the UK's counterterrorism police warned that the country would be at a heightened risk of terrorism for many years to come. Mr. Mark Rowley revealed that his department experienced many terror-related incidents during 2014: "We are facing a threat that is very different to what we have faced before in terms of its scale and nature, and at the moment the internet is a big part of that."[1]

Deputy leader of the UK's Labour Party, Mr. Khaled Mahmood, also expressed deep concern over the involvement of 2,000 UK jihadists in the sectarian conflict of the Middle East. He, however, criticized the government for its controversial border control mechanism. The borders of the country are not obstacles for jihadists returning home. A former police officer warned that people who sneaked under the police radar for jihad abroad were coming back through inadequate immigration controls at UK airports. The recent rise of ISIS in Syria, Iraq, Pakistan and Afghanistan, and its recruitment networks in Europe, caused a chain of counterterrorism measures in the UK.

---

[1] On November 26, 2014, *the UK's counterterrorism police* warned that the country would be at a heightened risk of terrorism for many years to come. Mr. Mark Rowley revealed that his department experienced many terror-related incidents during 2014

The UK and the European Union states have been increasingly anxious about their countries turning into domestic extremism and IS-recruiting hubs. "The increasing threat we face including from these so-called self-starting terrorists means that we should now go further in strengthening our capabilities," David Cameron told parliament.[1]

The government and law enforcement agencies are on the run; the Prime Minister himself is discontented over the intensified process of radicalization, while the Home Secretary is confused about how to tackle this hydra. Relations between the Home Office, Police Federation and Number-10 are in strains on many law and order management issues. The UK's mujahedeen are arriving here one by one, with new ideas, a fresh zeal and a brand new mentality from the training camps of the ISIS. They represent ISIS here and act on behalf of Abu Bakr al-Baghdadi. This is what Mark Rowley described as a different kind of threat in scale and nature. In view of these developments, the government announced new counterterrorism measures, including a range of powers to block suspected UK jihadists from returning home. The Home Office used to seek the cooperation of intelligence agencies to intercept possible terror attacks. The home secretary warned, "We are in the middle of a generational struggle against a deadly terrorist ideology."[2] She repeatedly described these points in her speech at the Royal United Services Institute for Strategic Studies:

> Since the start of this government, the counterterrorism internet referral unit has secured the removal of 65,000 items from the internet that encouraged or glorified acts of terrorism. More than 46,000 of these have been removed since December last year. At present, content relating to IS, Syria and Iraq represents around 70% of the unit's caseload. Since I became home secretary, I have excluded hundreds of people, in total, from the UK. I have excluded 61 people on national security grounds and 72 people because their presence here would not have been conducive to the public good. In

[1] *Daily Mail* 25 November 2014.
[2] Ibid.

total, I have excluded 84 hate preachers. Seventy-four organizations are at present proscribed because they are engaged in, or support, terrorism.[1]

The above-cited figures show how the growing networks of international terrorism and home-grown extremism are intensifying with each passing day. The situation is very complicated. One day, the government proposes one way of countering these threats and, another day, it changes its position. The home secretary recently told us, "When the security and intelligence agencies tell us that the threat we face is now more dangerous than at any time before or since 9/11, we should take notice. So the message to UK nationals participating in terrorism overseas is clear: 'You will only be allowed to come home on our terms.'" The issue though remains the same: neither the jihadists were not intercepted nor were they prosecuted.

The above-mentioned security analysis gives us an ugly picture of law and order in the country. There are discontents within the Home Office that raise serious questions about the professional mechanisms of Mrs. Teresa May's office. Recently, one of her Ministers resigned, criticizing her treatment of Liberal Democratic coalition colleagues. Due to the changing mechanism of terror and foreign-sponsored groups across the country, all 43 of the police forces, the Home Office and the law enforcement agencies continue to adopt a different code of conduct that causes a breakdown of trust amongst these agencies and the public at large. Moreover, the Foreign and Commonwealth Office issues a travel advisory in order to inform UK citizens that extremists might target them for their country's involvement in airstrikes against ISIS. All these statements and warnings from the Home Secretary, Prime Minister and counterterrorism officials show that they have failed to respond to this threatening situation professionally.

---

[1] *Daily Times,* 02 December 2014

CHAPTER 7. THE CHANGING FACE OF POLICING POLITICS, CLOSED CIRCUIT TV CAMERAS AND THE POLICING CULTURE IN BRITAIN

The Constitution of Britain is composed of laws and rules that create institutions and maintain the relationship between the state, individuals and among all institutions. The law is enforced by law enforcement agencies that tend to be limited to operating within a specific jurisdiction. In the UK, there are numerous policing organizations and their private partners struggling to enforce law and maintain order but everything is not going in the right direction in the policing community and community policing system. Relations between communities and the police are strained as they do not trust each other in the fight against terrorism, extremism and serious organized crime. In the last three years, the UK's law enforcement strategy is in deep crisis as frustration continues to exacerbate the pain of the Police Department, Home Office and policing intelligence agencies. Terror-related incidents increased, Islamic State (ISIS) recruited and radicalized elements returning to the UK by the day, and the issue of illegal immigrants has all started causing torment for the authorities.

Prime Minister (PM) David Cameron recently authorized an investigation into the illegal funds of UK-based extremist jihadist groups, while Foreign Secretary Philip Hammond dramatically revealed that more than 600 radicalized Britons had been intercepted going for jihad to Syria. "Approximately 800 have made it through since 2012, with half of them still thought to be inside the war torn country," Philip told The Telegraph. The Metropolitan Police are facing unprecedented difficulty in dealing with these jihadists and racism across the country. In 2011, the failure of the Metropolitan Police to manage and control criminal gangs and their violent actions on the streets of London raised serious questions about the competency and credibility of the force. To improve the operational capability and remove the prevailing misunderstanding regarding the police force, Mr. Tom Winsor had been assigned the task of conducting an independent review of police officers and staff remuneration and conditions, which was published on March 8, 2011.[1]

The Home Secretary once admitted that the Home Office had implemented the majority of Mr. Tom Winsor's recommendations, and further added that there were holes that needed to be tackled. After a thorough consideration and deep investigation of the case, Mr. Tom designed the modern police pay structure, which could not succeed. Police officers are still unable to manage their kitchens and mortgages with the shallow monthly amount they receive. The two years freeze on pay increments and hour allowance could not bring change to the minds of many officers. Mr. Tom Winsor's proposal to encourage young people to join the police force also proved ineffective. There is fear that foreign intelligence agents or criminal gangs may possibly infiltrate the police department by applying for employment.

In his 1,000-page report, Mr. Tom maintained that the roots of policing lie in a working class structure. This perception enraged thousands of police officers. Against these reforms, on July 24, 2012, the Police Negotiation Board did not agree to some proposals relating to pay and conditions, while Mr. Tom Winsor's

---

[1] Approximately 800 have made it through since 2012, with half of them still thought to be inside the war torn country, Philip told *The Telegraph*. The Metropolitan Police are facing unprecedented difficulty in dealing with these jihadists and racism across the country. In 2011, the failure of the Metropolitan Police to manage and control criminal gangs and their violent actions on the streets of London raised serious questions about the competency and credibility of the force. *The Guardian*, 15 January 2015, *Telegraph*, 15 January 2016-04-03

policing reforms faced strong opposition from some institutions and specific circles.[1]

In 2010, the coalition government in Britain announced a 20% reduction in the police budget over a period of four years, which prompted frustration within the force as many police forces began to consider outsourcing key service areas to the private sector to save money. In July 2012, the failure of the G4S in maintaining the Olympics' security generated negative debate in print and electronic media. The debate noted the inability of private security agencies to help the police in maintaining law and order in the country. In my recent book, *The Crisis of Britain's Surveillance State*, I indicated that private security companies have not adhered to national interests; their interests are with the money they are paid for. After reading these disappointing sagas of failed law enforcement strategies, one can understand the fear and irritation of our law enforcement agencies from the fact that due to their shrunk financial recourses, terrorists and foreign espionage networks across the country are making trouble.

The police department and Home Office maintain different priorities, while the priorities of intelligence agencies are quite different from both as they want stern action against domestic and international terrorist networks inside the country. Criminal gangs and Muslim extremists openly challenge the authority of the police and stab innocent citizens in the streets. The police are unable to tackle these outlawed criminals with empty hands. Corruption in the police department is a matter of great concern for the Home Office and Scotland Yard as well. In 2014, 3,000 allegations against the UK police were leveled but only 1,500 were investigated. The performance of the government's prevention strategy has been very poor during the last two years. Law enforcement agencies are still unable to infiltrate into the networks of foreign terrorist groups operating in the country. Some research reports recently highlighted a countrywide operation of foreign sponsored, serious organized crime and human trafficking networks in conjunction with spy networks challenging the authority of law enforcement agencies.[2]

---

[1] *Daily Times*, 19 January 2016
[2] In 2014, 3,000 allegations against the UK police were leveled but only 1,500 were investigated. The performance of the government's preven-

Mr. Edward Snowden exposed the inability of British agencies to intercept radicals joining Islamic State (ISIS). Hate crime, extremism, criminal gangs' networks and the presence of foreign intelligence networks across the country have threatened the lives of British citizens. Every day, we experience new incidents of violence and terrorism but British law enforcement agencies (though well-equipped) have been unable to respond professionally. To manage law and order, and effectively counter domestic and international terror networks, the government needs wide-ranging security sector reforms. Britons still need to learn and manage forces with a professional streak.

Closing hundreds of police stations may further deteriorate law and order across the country. There are some laws that remain ineffective while the government security threat level is at an all time high, but it has also been unsatisfactory. The Prime Minister has shown little interest in the deteriorating law and order in the country. The performance of police officers needs deep improvement and the police department needs a professional and educated police force. In view of the violent threat from ISIS and extremist groups in the country, Scotland Yard has doubled the number of armed police patrol. The Met will also boast a 400-strong specialist squad of firearm officers. The Scotland Yard chief, Sir Bernard Hogan-Howe, recently announced that he was increasing the total number of trained marksmen by six hundred.

The role of CCTV cameras in law enforcement is of great importance. These tools are making effective the policing way of operation in the streets and town of the United Kingdom. In fact, CCTV cameras identify crime scene and the action of criminals in streets and market to help the police in arresting anti social elements. In fact, CCTV cameras were installed in Britain to interdict burglary, robbery, assault, theft, fraud and other traditional crimes, but the use of these cameras become controversial when some communities complained that police uses CCTV against their privacy and social activities. According to the Home Office promotional booklet states that the CCTV can be a solution to racial harassment, drug use, sexual harassment

tion strategy has been very poor during the last two years. Law enforcement agencies are still unable to infiltrate into the networks of foreign terrorist groups operating in the country. 19 Jan 2016, *Daily Times*

and discrimination, but response of the public to this effort of the Home Office has not been positive since the installation of these surveillance cameras.[1]

Fundamentally, one cannot deny the benefits of CCTV cameras, but communities are not satisfied with performance of these cameras as terror-related incidents robbery, theft, sexual assaults, and attacks on minorities in buses and trains exacerbated, and the CCTV Cameras have failed to help the police in arresting criminals and racist elements. As I cited above that the CCTV Cameras have both positive and negative aspects in preventing crime, therefore, it also generate crime like the violation of privacy in houses and markets. If we read the details of the Cyber Security Strategy of the United Kingdom, we can find both positive and critical information about the function of CCTV Cameras. The Cyber Security Strategy acknowledges: "It is not possible to eliminate cyber crime."[2]

In another report, the BBC (2010) noted people's reservations on the function of CCTV Cameras. There are many complaints registered with the prevention of crime council that these cameras just generate fear among local communities and business firms. Muslim Communities in the UK often complained against the installation of CCTV Cameras in their areas by the police to monitor their religious ceremonies and private lives. They say this also generates misunderstanding between the government and communities. As per my observation, these security cameras are, in fact, an invasion on our privacy and private lives. The installations of these cameras in bathrooms and dressing rooms have no justification at all. Yes, the presence of CCTV is of much importance, and it plays a significant role in protecting public in streets and markets, but the unprofessional use has prompted some misunderstanding between the law enforcement agencies and communities.[3]

---

[1] *The Crisis of Britain's Surveillance State: Security, Law Enforcement and the Intelligence War in Cyberspace*, Musa Khan Jalalzai, Algora Publishing, New York, 2014. Also, *Issues Monitor Cyber Crime—A Growing Challenge for Governments*, John Herhalt, KPMG International, Volume, 08, July 2011.
[2] *CCTV Surveillance, Video Practices and Technology*, H Kruegle, Butterworth Heinemanne Books, 15 December 2006
[3] National Crime Prevention Council, available at: http://www.ncpc. org/about

If we look at the positive function of CCTV, we can find that CCTV reduce fear, help the police in investigation, provide technical assistance and gather information. Conversely, literature on the function of CCTV Cameras also noted their negative aspects involving displacement, increasing fear and the increase of crime reporting, which is an irksome issue for the police. In communities and markets, people response has been negative since long as they understand these cameras are spying on them. According to a second opinion, the CCTV may possibly increase in recording crime, which is not acceptable for the law enforcement agencies.[1]

The CCTV Cameras also causes of unintended effects, good and bad or false sense of security. Recent research reports have documented the negative aspects of CCTV Cameras and their inconclusive prevention capabilities. There are mixed opinions which demand change in the function of the CCTV and changes in surveillance law to make effective the function of these devices.[2]

Some suggest that the main issue is heavy cost on this business, needs to be reduced. Experts understand that the installation of these cameras across the country undermined the traditional concept of policing communities and community policing. They say that in majority crime reports made by CCTV, the police fail to analyze these reports in its true sense. They complain that the CCTV Cameras do not work properly, and criminals have baseball caps and hooded tops to hide their faces, and operate quickly. Security Cameras making people feel safe falsely, and the robbers robe their house with a modern technique.[3]

---

[1] The UK Cyber Security Strategy, November 2011, www.gov.uk/government/uploads/system/uploads/attachment_data/file/60961/uk-cyber-security-strategy-final.pdf, see also, The National Crime Prevention Council at: http://www.ncpc.org/about.

[2] *The UK Cyber Security Strategy, 2011,* and also *Cyber Crime and Cyber Security: Key Issues for the 2015 Parliament,* available at: www.parliament.uk/business/publications/research/key-issues-parliament-2015/defence-and-security/cyber-security/

[3] *The* CCTV site "Internet Eyes hope to catch criminals," Dhruti Shah, *BBC News,* 2010, also see, the College of Policing, http://library.college.police.uk/docs/what-works/What-works-briefing-effects-of-CCTV-2013.pdf.

The increasing use of CCTV Cameras in public domain risk changing the mind of communities about the government attitude towards minorities across the UK. They see these cameras in their areas as an act of discrimination and violation of their privacy. The UK Surveillance Commissioner, and a former senior counterterrorism officer, Toney Porter warned in his recent interview that the police monitoring of people must be in a transparent manner.[1]

On 22 October 2015, in his speech to the Association of Police and Crime Commissioners in London, Surveillance Camera Commissioner, Tony Porter said: "So, there is a disconnect here-in some areas CCTV is valued as an excellent tool for policing elsewhere it's dismissed. I often hear from local authorities CCTV mangers that they never get any feedback from forces on how effective CCTV has been in aiding investigations, arrests, and convictions. How can they evidence its value to their counselors with ever diminishing budget if they are getting no feedback on its effectiveness? How do they know their cameras aren't fit for purpose if no one tells them"?[2]

Majority of the CCTV Cameras have failed to deliver properly as we have experience in the past when criminal robbed many houses in East and West London by applying new criminal techniques. The irony is that majority of business and other firms and systems little invested in the duplicate signed copies, sealed evidence bags and others to provide the court with an unbroken chain of evidence. Second, the times and date stamp on the CCTV monitor printout can be fabricated in personal computers because video editing tools are easily available in the market.[3]

Now amid controversies and complaints, the Information Commissioner's Office (ICO) issued code practice of surveillance under the Data Protection Act 1998, which covers the use

---

[1] The Centre for Problem-Oriented Policing, www.Popcenter.org and also *The Crisis of Britain's Surveillance State: Security, Law Enforcement and the Intelligence War in Cyberspace*, Musa Khan Jalalzai, Algora Publishing, New York, 2014.
[2] "The effect of CCTV on Public Safety: Research Roundup," *Journalist's Resource*, 11 February 2014, and also *Journal of Quantitative Criminology*, Volume 30, Issue 2, June 2014
[3] *Why Surveillance Cameras Don't Reduce Crime*, 31 March 2005, Clive Robinson

of CCTV. The code was updated in 2008 to bring about concordance between the government and communities. It is estimated that there are millions CCTV Cameras operating in the UK, including 750,000 in sensitive locations but the graph of crime and crime-related activities is still there.[1]

The emergence of surveillance technology has confined human being to a limited space. As the criminal culture in the United Kingdom prevailed during the last 15 years, the demand for the CCTV Cameras increased. Now, in spite of its benefits, discussion about their negative impacts diverted the attention of Crime Commissioner and law enforcement authorities toward its professional use. In the United Kingdom, CCTV help the police in fighting crime, but sometimes, CCTV fail to identify robbers and serious organized criminals.[2]

Moreover, the CCTV Cameras are also eroding our standing democratic right of privacy. In Markets, many companies believe the use of CCTV may help in improvement of their employee's behaviors, but it also creates ill will between the companies' owners and employees. People complain that the CCTV Cameras are harmful to their life and privacy. They say that as they are being protected by CCTV, they also feel that they are watched everywhere.[3] The House of Commons Home affairs Committee on Counterterrorism in its report (2014–2015) on foreign fighters suggested a 5-point plan to strengthen the measures already in place:

1. Improve communication

Communication between the police, schools and parents is in need of vast improvement. The police must engage in a regular and open dialogue with schools and community groups to ensure that information is exchanged and new initiatives can

---

[1] "UK Public Must Wake Up to Risks of CCTV, Says Surveillance Commissioner, Tony Porter," Matthew Weaver, *The Guardian*, 06 January 2015, details available at: http://www.theguardian.com/world/2015/jan/06/tony-porter-surveillance-commissioner-risk-cctv-public-transparent

[2] *The Maximum Surveillance Society: The Rise of CCTV*, Gary Armstrong, Clive Norris, Bloomsbury, September 1999

[3] Speech to the Association of Police and Crime Commissioners, Mr. Porter outlined PCC's statutory responsibilities in relation to Surveillance Cameras Code of Practice. 22 October 2015

be explored at community level. Schools and the police must inform parents immediately, and work together when there is even the smallest hint of radicalization, or a close association with someone who is thought to have been radicalized.

2. Increase police diversity

Dal Babu, former Chief Superintendent at the Metropolitan Police, raised concerns about diversity of officers involved in the Prevent program, arguing that "If you are going to fight terrorism effectively then your key operatives need to reflect the people that you are dealing with and that is not happening here." Assistant Commissioner Mark Rowley said in evidence to the Committee that he wants the counter-terrorism command to be "reflective of London," namely "40% from different minority groups" and that they have changed their recruitment criteria to be more reflective of London." It is essential that the officers working on the Prevent programme, as in other areas of the police, are truly reflective and representative of British society.

3. Provide advice

There needs to be an advice service open to all, particularly targeted at parents who wish to seek advice or express concerns about a particular individual. This must be well publicized, and be a less extreme step than using the Anti-Terrorist Hotline. There is a fear of stigmatization among communities and such a helpline could go some way in changing these attitudes. This method should be included in the Prevent strategy.

4. Provide a counter-narrative

The universality of the internet has enabled people to be radicalized in their bedrooms unnoticed by others. Policing social media sites such as Twitter, a means by which many IS propaganda has been spread for example, is impossible. Young people need to be equipped with the skills to become critical consumers of online content, in order to build a more natural resistance against radicalization through online extremist content and propaganda. This is not just about counter-radicalization: an informed, critical and questioning approach to online sources is a valuable asset in all aspects of a young person's social and intellectual development.

5. Improve international co-operation

According to the Turkish Ambassador, the British embassy in Ankara sent details about the girls to the Ministry of Foreign Affairs six days after the girls left the country. This is an unacceptably slow response which significantly reduced any chances of intercepting the girls on their journey while there was still time. International efforts to work in unison to tackle the growing number of young people travelling to these conflict zones to join extremist groups must be strengthened urgently. (House of Commons Home Affairs Committee Counter-terrorism: foreign fighters Nineteenth Report of Session 2014–15, five point plan)[1]

---

[1] The Information Commissioner Office website details about surveillance c=ameras, 21 May2015, available at: ,https://www.ico.org.uk/media/for-organisations/documents/1542/cctv-code-of-practice.pdf.The House of Commons Home affairs Committee on Counterterrorism in its report (2014-2015) on foreign fighters suggested a five-point plan to strengthen the measures already in place

CHAPTER 8. INTELLIGENCE SURVEILLANCE, RADICALIZATION, LAW ENFORCEMENT AND THE THREAT OF TERRORISM AND EXTREMISM IN BRITAIN

The US and UK are under severe criticism from domestic and international privacy and human rights groups on their pushy methods of intelligence surveillance and spying on their own citizens. The CIA, National Security Agency (NSA) and Government Communications Headquarters' (GCHQ's) recent way of interception communication have been deeply irksome to families and business communities in both countries. The GCHQ's interception of the fiber-optic cable network, which is the digital equivalent of opening all the mail going in and out of the UK, has become a central debate in print and electronic media. In the US, the issue of surveillance is also hot.

On 27 August, 2013, notwithstanding civilian complaints against the violation of their privacy, President Barack Obama announced the Review Group on Intelligence and Communications Technologies (RGICT), which was welcomed only by his friends while the majority members of civil society remained critical. During my study with the University of Stanford, California, and University of Maryland, Washington DC, I experienced many new things about the operations of intelligence surveillance and geospatial intelligence mechanism in the US.

What is happening behind the curtain is quite disturbing.[1]

After the 9/11 terrorist attacks, former President Bush introduced the controversial Patriot Act, which caused many problems in and outside the country. Section 215 of the Surveillance Act was amended, which demands the business record, while the Foreign Intelligence Surveillance Act (FISA) did not grant the government any authority to compel the production of such records. There are contradictions and many flaws in the US's intelligence surveillance system, which continue to alienate the citizens from the state. Not all things are going in the right direction with the operational method of Executive Order 12333, Sections 215 and 702 of the Surveillance Act. FISA is not the only legal authority governing foreign intelligence activities; other statutes and executive orders also spread blankets, covering other facets of intelligence operations.[2]

Executive Order 12333 is the strongest pillar of surveillance under FISA, but many questions arise about its method of operation and implementation. According to a report by the President's Review Group (2013) on Intelligence and Communications Technologies:

> With respect to National Security Agency (NSA), for example, Executive Order 12333 designates NSA as the manager for Signals Intelligence (SIGINT) for the intelligence community and the attorney general's guidelines define how SIGINT may be conducted for collection activities not governed by FISA." The NSA locates targets for lethal drone strikes while a majority of Taliban and Islamic State (IS) commanders protect-

---

[1] "Liberty and Security in a Changing World," Report and Recommendations of *The President's Review Group on Intelligence and Communications Technologies*, 12 December 2013, https://www.whitehouse.gov/sites/default/files/docs/2013-12-12_rg_final_report.pdf.

[2] Section 215 of the Surveillance Act was amended, which demands the business record, while the Foreign Intelligence Surveillance Act (FISA) did not grant the government any authority to compel the production of such records. There are contradictions and many flaws in the US's intelligence surveillance system, which continue to alienate the citizens from the state. Not all things are going in the right direction with the operational method of Executive Order 12333, Sections 215 and 702 of the Surveillance Act, Electronic Privacy Information Centre, https://epic.org/privacy/surveillance/12333/.

ing themselves from the NSA purposely distribute different SIM cards among their fighters in order to elude their trackers. When they go to meetings, they take out their SIM cards, put them in a bag and mix them up. Executive Order 12333, which instructs intelligence agencies to collect information and data, notes: "Accurate and timely information about the capabilities, intentions and activities of foreign powers, organizations or persons and their agents is essential to informed decision making in the areas of national defense and foreign relations.[1]

In the UK, we are living under open skies and a shining moon, exposed badly to everyone. Our privacy has become a joke as our surveillance system (TEMPORA) is evolving with different faces. We are more exposed than the US. In the UK, there are dozens of surveillance laws, reverberations and the big drum (TEMPORA), which has many eyes, hears us with dozens of ears, and watches us from a distance. It also has the membership of Five Eyes, an intelligence alliance between Australia, the US, Canada, New Zealand and the UK. In 2015, here in the UK, the Investigatory Powers Tribunal (IPT) termed the regulations covering access by Britain's GCHQ to emails and phone records intercepted by the NSA as A breach of the human rights law:

> This is a historic victory in the age-old battle for the right to privacy and free expression," said Rachel Logan, Amnesty International UK's legal program director. Until last year, this way of stealing data and information from email was illegal but, this year, UK surveillance agencies started violating surveillance and human rights laws with impunity. This is the critical judgment

---

[1] According to a report by the President's Review Group (2013) on Intelligence and Communications Technologies: "With respect to National Security Agency (NSA), for example, Executive Order 12333 designates NSA as the manager for Signals Intelligence (SIGINT) for the intelligence community and the attorney general's guidelines define how SIGINT may be conducted for collection activities not governed by FISA. "The NSA Report: Liberty and Security in a Changing World," The President's Review Group on Intelligence and Communications Technologies, Richard A. Clarke, Michael J. Morell, Geoffrey R. Stone, Cass R. Sunstein, Peter Swire, Princeton University Press, 31 Mar 2014.

of the IPT since its inception in 2000. According to the IPT argument, "The regime governing the soliciting, receiving, storing and transmitting by UK authorities of private communications of individuals located in the UK, which have been obtained by US authorities contravened Articles 8 or 10 of the European convention on human rights.[1]

In 2013, newspapers reported the GCHQ routine intercept of submarine fiber-optic cables containing the private communications of millions of UK residents. A recent research report by the Don't Spy on Us Campaign noted:

> The Snowden revelations regarding the scope of GCHQ surveillance under TEMPORA have highlighted the use of warrants for the interception of so-called 'external communications' under section 8(4) RIPA (Regulations of Investigatory Power Act, 2000. It is now clear that section 8(4) warrants have been used as the basis for the mass interception by the GCHQ of millions of private communications as well as its bulk collection of communications data.[2]

On February 16, 2015, interestingly, the Guardian reported that a man from Liverpool had been charged with attempting to obtain a chemical weapon. The 31-year-old Muslim was arrested following a joint raid by the North West Counterterrorism Unit (NWCTU) and Merseyside police. Muhammad Ammer Ali of Prescott Road, Liverpool, was produced at the Westminster magistrate's court on February 17, 2015. He was accused of attempting to have a chemical weapon in his possession between 10 January and 12 February 2015, contrary to the Criminal Attempts Act, 1981 and the Chemical Weapons Act, 1996. Police seized a number of items during searches at five addresses in Merseyside on February 11. Now the question is: notwithstanding the multifaceted surveillance from the skies and on the earth, and the blanket of TEMPORA, why had this man been in possession of chemical weapons for the last two months? The an-

---

[1] *Daily Times*, 03 March 2015.
[2] Ibid.

swer is that many things are not going in the right direction in the UK.[1]

In the UK, every year, the fluctuation of our security threat level become questionable when new jihadist networks are introduced to communities here. These security threat levels remain irksome as we have been unable to tackle the threat of radicalization and extremism. They are sometimes high, sometimes potential and sometimes severe, but no permanent solution has been sought to professionally tackle threatening ideologies. We are living in fear and do not feel secure as these elements are openly dancing in our streets.

They are also involved in serious organized crime to generate funds for the military operations conducted by the Islamic State of Iraq and Syria (ISIS), the Taliban or Lashkar-e-Tayyaba (LeT). Organized crime has also deeply affected our financial market while the National Crime Agency (NCA) and police have failed to prevent narco-smugglers and criminal mafia groups from ruining the lives of our communities across the country. The issue is very serious as jihadists are returning from Syria, Iraq, Afghanistan, Pakistan and Bangladesh with a new zeal and radicalized Salafist ideology. There are 500 UK citizens fighting for ISIS. The man who beheaded a US journalist, a UK national in Iraq, was one of them.

We have another newly converted man who beheaded an 82-year-old woman in London in 2015. This was a new Taliban-style killing tradition introduced to the UK recently. This way of killing frightens the entire population. With the arrival of these radicalized young jihadists and perhaps the awakening of jihadists already associated with the sleeper networks of international terrorist and domestic extremist groups, security and law enforcement agencies will face the real ordeal of maintaining stability in the near future. The changing threat level, the return of control order and the new amendment to the national security document indicate that the government has failed to tackle

---

[1] On February 16, 2015, interestingly, *The Guardian* reported that a man from Liverpool had been charged with attempting to obtain a chemical weapon. The 31-year-old Muslim was arrested following a joint raid by the North West Counterterrorism Unit (NWCTU) and Merseyside police. Muhammad Ammer Ali of Prescott Road, Liverpool, was produced at the Westminster magistrate's court on February 17, 2015.

the crisis of domestic radicalization. Short term fixes and patch-up jobs are not enough. Real zeal and real solutions are urgently needed.

The National Security Strategy (NSS) has given priority to counterterrorism and information warfare but there is a gap between the priorities of the government and the private sector. In order to meet the needs of the private sector, the government must create policies to combat the changing security threat in our country. In 2011, the government updated the strategy of counterterrorism that focuses on four specific areas.[1] The strategy stresses the need to stop terror attacks and the people who support them. The four key areas are: pursue, prevent, protect and prepare (PPPP). After the killing of a British soldier in East London, priorities changed and a new counterterrorism strategy was introduced to tackle domestic radicalization. Prime Minister David Cameron introduced a new strategy called the Tackling Extremism and Radicalization Task Force (TERFOR) but it failed to deliver.

The latest police statistics show that young people continue to make up a disproportionately high number of those arrested for terrorist-related offences and of those travelling to join terrorist groups in Syria and Iraq. Prime Minister David Cameron noted, "I said in July that tackling extremism will be the struggle of our generation, one which we will defeat if we work together. All public institutions have a role to play in rooting out and challenging extremism. It is not about oppressing free speech or stifling academic freedom, it is about making sure that radical views and ideas are not given the oxygen they need to flourish. Schools, universities and colleges, more than anywhere else, have a duty to protect impressionable young minds and ensure that our young people are given every opportunity to reach their potential. That is what our one nation government is focused on delivering."

The Prime Minister was to receive regular updates from departments on how these proposals are being implemented to provide a comprehensive approach to dealing with extremism. The members of the Extremism Taskforce were:

---

[1] *Daily Times*, 12 September 2014.

1. The Prime Minister (chair)
2. The Deputy Prime Minister
3. The Chancellor of the Exchequer
4. The Secretary of State for the Home Department
5. The Secretary of State for Business, Innovation and Skills
6. The Lord Chancellor and Secretary of State for Justice
7. The Secretary of State for Education
8. The Secretary of State for Communities and Local Government
9. The Minister for Schools
10. The Minister for Faith and Communities
11. The Minister for Government Policy (Policy Paper, 04 December 2013).

The new legislation is certainly necessary, but the draft bill, while moving fractionally in the right direction, has serious flaws. The government tried to bring its multitudinous powers together in a single bill. In this it has failed, with a number of important powers still lying outside the scope of the checks and oversights proposed under the draft legislation. The supposed strength of the new legislation is its "double lock" authorization process, with both ministerial and judicial approval required for the grant of any warrant. However, the decision to retain the home secretary's authorization process for domestic interception—the first lock of the double lock—is utterly irrational.[1]

Domestic interception should not be a political decision. In any event, this system does not offer any accountability, as ministers never answer questions on security and certainly never admit to security errors. Even with surveillance powers other than domestic interception, the proposed "double lock" falls far short of what is needed, and fails to live up to government promises. Limiting judicial commissioners to considering warrants on judicial review principles means they can overrule a home secretary only if he or she is deemed to have acted utterly unreasonably. The government has hamstrung the process, in essence turning it into a judicial rubber stamp.

On 01 July 2015, the Investigatory Powers Tribunal (IPT), which investigates complaints of unlawful contact by the UK in-

---

[1] Ibid.

telligence agencies, notified Amnesty International that UK government agencies had spied on the organization by intercepting, accessing and storing its communications. The IPT previously identified one of two NGOs which it found had been subjected to unlawful surveillance by the UK government as the Egyptian Initiative for Personal Rights (EIPR), when it should have said Amnesty. The other NGO which was spied on was the Legal Resources Centre in South Africa. The UK surveillance agency GCHQ has been officially censured for not revealing enough about how it shares information with its American counterparts. The Investigatory Powers Tribunal said GCHQ failed until December 2014 to make clear enough details of how it shared data from mass internet surveillance. It was the IPT's first ruling against an intelligence agency in its 15-year history. The Home Office said the government was "committed to transparency.¹

In December the IPT ruled that the system of UK intelligence collection did not breach the European Convention of Human Rights, following a complaint by campaign groups including Privacy International and Liberty. But the tribunal has now ruled that the system did "contravene" human rights law-until extra information was made public in December. In its disclosures in December, GCHQ said UK intelligence services were "permitted" to request information gathered by Prism and Upstream - US surveillance systems which can collect information on "non-US persons.²

Complaints against the surveillance mechanism of Government Communication Headquarters (GCHQ), and its joint operation with the EU intelligence agencies in print and electronic media raised several questions including the violation the right of privacy of the citizens of the continent. In the past, Several intelligence agencies of France, Germany, Sweden and many other states developed ways of mass surveillance in close partnership

---

¹ The IPT previously identified one of two NGOs which it found had been subjected to unlawful surveillance by the UK government as the Egyptian Initiative for Personal Rights (EIPR), when it should have said Amnesty. *Amnesty International*, 03 July 2015
² GCHQ said UK intelligence services were "permitted" to request information gathered by Prism and Upstream-US surveillance systems which can collect information on "non-US persons,' BBC, 06 February 2015

with the GCHQ to monitor the movement of their citizens, and intercept what they understand is a threat to national security. A loose but growing eavesdropping alliance allowed intelligence agencies from one country to cultivate ties with corporations from another to facilitate the trawling of the web, according to GCHQ documents leaked by the former US intelligence contractor Edward Snowden.

Writer Julian Borger (2013) in one of his recent article noted the mass surveillance alliance of GCHQ with EU agencies: "However, in a country-by-country survey of its European partners, GCHQ officials expressed admiration for the technical capabilities of German intelligence to do the same thing. The survey in 2008, when TEMPORA was being tested, said the Federal Intelligence Service (BND), had "huge technological potential and good access to the heart of the internet – they are already seeing some bearers running at 40Gbps and 100Gbps. Bearers is the GCHQ term for the fiber optic cables, and gigabits per second (Gbps) measures the speed at which data runs through them. Four years after that report, GCHQ was still only able to monitor 10 Gbps cables, but looked forward to tap new 100 Gbps bearers eventually."

Mr. Julian Borger further discusses the expanding partnership of GCHQ with the intelligence surveillance agencies of EU member states: "In the case of the Spanish intelligence agency, the National Intelligence Centre (CNI), the key to mass internet surveillance, at least back in 2008, was the Spaniards' ties to a British telecommunications company (again unnamed. Corporate relations are among the most strictly guarded secrets in the intelligence community). That was giving them "fresh opportunities and uncovering some surprising results. "GCHQ has not yet engaged with CNI formally on IP exploitation, but the CNI have been making great strides through their relationship with a UK commercial partner. GCHQ and the commercial partner have been able to coordinate their approach. The commercial partner has provided the CNI some equipment whilst keeping us informed, enabling us to invite the CNI across for IP-focused discussions this autumn," the report said. It concluded that GCHQ "have found a very capable counterpart in CNI, particularly in the field of Covert Internet Ops"

Some intelligence reports also indicate that the use of electronic surveillance practices that go beyond traditional, targeted surveillance for intelligence purposes in five EU member states like the UK, Sweden, France, Germany and the Netherlands received deep criticism for their violation of privacy rights across Europe. In principal, the UK legal framework allows TEMPORA only to target 'external' communications, in other words communications between non-UK residents, or between a UK resident and a non-UK resident. Reports concerning the logistical operation of the TEMPORA programme imply some cooperation with private-sector telecommunications companies.

The ruling by the Investigatory Powers Tribunal responsible for monitoring the UK secret services against the GCHQ's access to private communications received a good support in civil society. The Investigatory Powers Tribunal (IPT) ruled that the agency's access to intercepted information obtained by the US National Security Agency (NSA) breached human rights law. However, spy agencies across Western Europe are working together on mass surveillance of Internet and phone traffic comparable to programs run by their U.S. counterpart denounced by European governments, the Guardian reported. The Guardian named Germany, France, Spain, Sweden and the Netherlands as countries where intelligence agencies had been developing such methods in cooperation with counterparts including Britain's surveillance agency GCHQ.

The one and half year inquiry by the intelligence and security committee of parliament (ISC) found that the existing laws are not being broken by the agencies and insisted that GCHQ's bulk interception does not amount to bulk surveillance. The inquiry was prompted by the revelations from former CIA contractor turned whistleblower Edward Snowden. The committee concluded that there was no bulk surveillance and gave a lengthy defense on it:

> We have established that bulk interception cannot be used to search for and examine the communications of an individual in the UK unless GCHQ first obtain a specific authorization naming that individual, signed by a secretary of state."[1]

---

[1] The inquiry was prompted by the revelations from former CIA con-

Extremist and radicalized elements continue to participate in overseas jihadist operations. Moreover, the PPPP strategy has also failed to intercept UK jihadists from joining ISIS and Taliban networks. The scale of danger posed by extremists in and outside the country was underlined when jihadists threatened to kill non-Muslims in the streets of the UK. The returnees will be kept under surveillance as the government still looks for a community based de-radicalization program. How is it possible, then, that the government has never consulted communities on counterterrorism strategies and law enforcement mechanisms?

In addition, last year, the government was also thinking on different lines to restore the power to issue control orders (an order issued by the Home Secretary to protect the public by restricting an individual's liberty if he is deemed a terrorist risk.). The idea of the control order has already failed. Unless these extremist returnees are de-radicalized on the community level, no TERFOR or control order can stop them from joining the ISIS terrorist network. Moreover, we also face the threat of cyber terrorism. This threat is violent and damaging. No doubt, the GCHQ is the best professional intelligence agency but we are unable to counter the threat of Chinese, Russian or Indian cyber attacks as we still need to recruit young information warriors. They have established strong cyber forces respectively that use modern technologies of the kind we do not have.

When we failed to counter cyber attacks professionally, we made more amendments to cyber laws and Computer Misuse Act, under which hackers who threaten the UK's national security face life imprisonment. The fact of the matter is that hackers or cyber warriors target us from a safe distance. How can we arrest them? We need to undermine those who target us from within the country. The UK Cyber Security Strategy (2011) also notes that cyber threats come from other states that seek to conduct espionage with the aim of spying on or compromising our government, military, industrial and economic assets, as well as monitoring opponents of their own regimes. The threat to national security has intensified as information warriors directly challenge us. The UK Home Office's recently reported: "A major

---

tractor turned whistleblower Edward Snowden, *The Guardian*, 12 March 2015.

cyber attack on essential networks such as the national grid, police computers or supermarkets distribution systems could trigger severe social disruption."[1]

Under the new Serious Crime Bill, cyber attacks that cause loss of life, serious illness, injury, or serious damage to national security will carry a life sentence. Moreover, cyber attacks that cause environmental and financial damage will carry a 14-year prison sentence. The irony is that we have failed to arrest a single cyber terrorist so far, while professional cyber warriors continue to establish their networks here and target state institutions. We are already facing a new kind of intelligence war in the UK that targets our institutions from a safe distance. We also face the threat of nuclear terrorism. Extremists and terrorists can gain access to nuclear materials like uranium and plutonium to make an improvised explosive device and use it against our critical infrastructure. In fact, the threat of the availability of nuclear material has intensified as technologies and capabilities proliferate. We can easily find ourselves in a far more dangerous world.

Prospect of an intelligence war in Britain

The recent revelations of US whistleblower Edward Snowden exacerbated the possibilities of an intelligence war between European states that look at each other with suspicion. Germany cancelled its Cold War era pact with the UK while European intelligence agencies became more vigilant about UK intelligence tactics. The National Security Agency (NSA) and the UK Government Communications Headquarters (GCHQ) had prepared a comprehensive list of individuals and institutions including the European competition commissioner, buildings and NGOs that provide financial assistance to Africa. Brussels reacted furiously to claim that the NSA and GCHQ spied on the European commissioner.[2]

---

[1] The UK Cyber Security Strategy (2011) also notes that cyber threats come from other states that seek to conduct espionage with the aim of spying on or compromising our government, military, industrial and economic assets, as well as monitoring opponents of their own regimes. Home Office Report, *The Telegraph*, London, 04 June 2014

[2] *The Crisis of Britain Surveillance state* and also *The Guardian*, 01 August 2013.

The European commissioner has access to highly confiden-tial commercial information. The commissioner's spokeswoman has said, "This is not the type of behavior that we expect from strategic partners, let alone from our own member states." Now, the EU has decided to create its own intelligence agency by be-ginning the development of surveillance drones and spy satel-lites. The Italian prime minister attacked British Prime Minister David Cameron over allegations that the UK intercepted secret Italian communications and then passed them on to the NSA. The latest revelations from Edward Snowden show that the NSA and GCHQ spied on 100 top officials from 60 states, in-cluding the Israeli prime minister, European policy makers and several aid groups.

The intelligence war between Indian and Pakistani intel-ligence agencies across the United Kingdom, particularly, in London has caused complex security challenges. There is specu-lation that Pakistani intelligence agencies shamelessly follow, target and harass writers and journalists in streets and towns, and those who criticize the policies of their state, while Afghan intelligence do the same. The networks of these agencies are deep and strong as they do whatever they want without fear. They have employed British citizens and instruct them on differ-ent directions. Those who visit Indian embassy or their cultural centers, and those who visit Pakistan embassy, these agencies become alert and translate their action into a violent action, but our agencies watch these illegal acts helplessly. Not only these, there are various foreign agencies involved in illegal activities.

Ninety-five percent of the UK citizens have no knowledge of the function of dozens secret intelligence units of their country. One of these secret units is an electronic intelligence unit that is responsible for surveillance; electronic propaganda campaign fo-cuses on law enforcement mechanism and counterterrorism op-erations. The Joint Threat Research Intelligence Group (JTRIG) is helping law enforcement agencies, including Met Police, MI5, Serious Organized Crime Agency (SOCA), Border Agency, Rev-enue and Customs (HMRC), and National Public Order and Intelligence Unit (NPOIU). Researchers Glenn Greenwald and Andrew Fishman (22 June 2015) have deeply analyzed the secret operational mechanism of this unit and elucidated many aspects of its revolving operational mechanism:

Documents published today by The Intercept demonstrate how the Joint Threat Research Intelligence Group (JTRIG), a unit of the signals intelligence agency Government Communications Headquarters (GCHQ), is involved in efforts against political groups it considers "extremist," Islamist activity in schools, the drug trade, online fraud and financial scams. Though its existence was secret until last year, JTRIG quickly developed a distinctive profile in the public understanding, after documents from NSA whistleblower Edward Snowden revealed that the unit had engaged in "dirty tricks" like deploying sexual "honey traps" designed to discredit targets, launching denial-of-service attacks to shut down Internet chat rooms, pushing veiled propaganda onto social networks and generally warping discourse online.[1]

On 13 June 2013, Washington Post and the Guardian published important stories about the leaked information by Edward Snowden, which exposed the US and UK secret data gathering mechanism through PRISM, UPSTREAM and TEMPORA. After these revelations, simply, the UK intelligence committee declared that the allegations that GCHQ had acted illegally by accessing the content of private communications via the PRISM programme were "unfounded." In 2015, the ISC conducted inquiry into the capabilities of electronic intelligence in intrusive techniques. The Intelligence Committee concluded that the existing legal framework governing these capabilities was unnecessarily complicated, and recommended that it be replaced with a new Act of Parliament.

On 09 February 2016, in his Daily Dot article, Eric Geller noted the power mechanism if GCHQ in data collection: "GCHQ can collect "external" communications in bulk under a section 8(4) warrant. It can then search for and select communications to examine using a selector of an individual who is overseas, providing the Secretary of State has certified this as necessary for

---

[1] Controversial GCHQ Unit Engaged in Domestic Law Enforcement, On Line Propaganda, *Psychology Research*, Glenn Greenwald, Andrew Fishman, June 22 2015

statutory purposes. If GCHQ wants to search for and select "external" communications to examine based on a selector of an individual in the UK, they must get additional authorization from a Secretary of State which names that person. The Secretary of State cannot issue section 8(1) or section 8(4) warrants unless they believe it is both necessary and proportionate."

In January 2016, Reprieve, an international human rights organization, reported that members of the UK's Parliamentary intelligence watchdog will not be allowed access to all intelligence or defense information relating to the new British practice of targeted killing by drone. David Cameron was asked by Andrew Tyrie MP whether the Intelligence and Security Committee (ISC) would be allowed to examine the military aspect of the targeted killing program, and whether he would commit to the Committee's security-cleared members being able to see all the relevant intelligence. According to the Reprieve report, Mr. Cameron refused on both points, stating that the ISC's job was to examine intelligence, not military affairs, and that he could not give the commitment Mr. Tyrie asked for regarding the Committee's access to intelligence. Mr. Tyrie pointed out that what the Committee is allowed to see remains under the control of the Secretary of State, and that its work on targeted killing "could be rendered meaningless" if it were barred from looking at the military operation.

Amidst these controversies, Prime Minister David Cameron visited Washington to further promote UK cyber skills. On 15 May 2015, Russian Television (RT) reported a select band of UK cyber-defense companies accompanied David Cameron in this trip. The 12 UK firms discussed joint proposals with the Obama administration. the Wall Street Journal reported Cameron's plan to ask the President face-to-face to criticize US tech companies such as Microsoft, Facebook, Google and Apple who, post-Snowden, have started to encrypt their communications by default. The British government quietly re-wrote the law to permit its electronic intelligence agency to continue with controversial surveillance practices, according to campaigners. In a statement, Privacy International said: "The government has quietly ushered through legislation amending the anti-hacking laws to exempt GCHQ from prosecution. Privacy International and other parties were notified of these just hours prior to a hearing of their claim against GCHQ's illegal hacking operations in the Investigatory Powers Tribunal."

Since the first reporting on documents disclosed by Edward Snowden in June 2013, a number of challenges to GCHQ's surveillance practices have been initiated in the UK. Today, in response to one of those applications, from Liberty and several other organizations, the court that oversees the GCHQ ruled against the UK intelligence services for the first time in its controversial 15 year history. In the short, two-page ruling, the Investigatory Powers Tribunal declared that, before December 2014 "the regime governing the soliciting, receiving, storing and transmitting by the UK authorities of private communications of individuals in the UK, which have been obtained by the US authorities" under the NSA's PRISM and UPSTREAM (collection from fiber-optic cable) programs breached Articles 8 and 10 of the European Convention on Human Rights.

These illegal interventions of the US and UK governments in the privacy of European states created a climate of mistrust across the continent, while Germany strongly protested against the UK spying on its institutions. In the UK, parliamentarians and politicians expressed deep concern over the complaints of European leaders against the UK's intelligence politics. In 2014, the UK's three chiefs of the intelligence agencies—MI5, MI6, and GCHQ — appeared before the Intelligence and Security Committee to explain the way intelligence operates. The US and UK are members of the Five-Eye intelligence sharing alliance, including Australia, New Zealand and Canada, but their method of surveillance clearly violates the principles of the alliance. French intelligence is cooperating with the Five Eyes alliance by systematically providing them with information. Sweden, Israel and Italy are also cooperating with the NSA and GCHQ.[1]

The Intelligence and Security Committee (ISC) was established in 1994, to oversee the expenditures of MI5, MI6 and GCHQ. It was reformed through the Justice and Intelligence Act

---

[1] The US and UK are members of the Five-Eye intelligence sharing alliance, including Australia, New Zealand and Canada, but their method of surveillance clearly violates the principles of the alliance. *Daily Times,* 07 January 2014

2013. Normally, national oversight practices vary greatly in term of how much power is granted to intelligence services, and how they are accountable for their actions. In most European states, democratic accountability of intelligence agencies is of great importance. Executive control, parliamentary oversight, judicial review, internal control and independent scrutiny are the ways democratic accountability is ensured. As a multicultural society, Britain has established a wide-ranging intelligence infrastructure to tackle extremism and international terrorism. Over the past forty years, specifically, technological advancement confined human being to limited activities. With this advancement, the power of the state also increased to carry out surveillance upon its citizens.

Knowledge and surveillance management compared to policing policy, has received surprisingly considerable attention. Intelligence has always been of much importance for security and law enforcement agencies. With the introduction of Special Arish Branch in 1883, the work of intelligence has been central in the operations of many police operational units in the country. Intelligence is a well-classified, analyzed and processed knowledge, which plays important role in the preparation of security plans of a state. Intelligence is knowledge, a decision oriented and action oriented knowledge. Without decision oriented knowledge and action oriented knowledge, no knowledge and information can help security agencies in the protection of state security. Intelligence has many forms, like national intelligence, strategic intelligence, tactical intelligence, signal intelligence, signature intelligence and foreign intelligence.[1]

Having provided accurate analytical information to the state and government, intelligence pinpoints the level of internal and external threats. Secret agencies (MI5 and MI6, GCHQ, DIS, JIC, CID, NIM, BI, Special Branch) in Britain have a brilliant record of over one hundred years. Special Branch, that played important role in the first and second world wars, was established in 1883.6 There are three other important intelligence agencies in the United Kingdom, known as MI5, MI6 and GCHQ, pro-

---

[1] *The Guardian*, 08 March 2013: The powers that allow British's intelligence agencies to spy on individuals, including foreign diplomats, were set out in the 1994 Intelligence Services Act (ISA).

tecting the national security of the country. All these agencies are working under Intelligence Act 1994, Security Service Acts 1989 and 1996. Established in 1909, MI6 is working as foreign intelligence, responsible to the foreign office of the country. MI6 gather information overseas. Another well reputed secret service, MI5, established in 1909, is operating under the 1994 Intelligence Act, working closely with the local police.[1]

Britain's intelligence agencies cannot do their job without the consent of their masters. Their hands are tied with Ministerial rope. Richard M. Bennett and Katie Bennett in their well-written report on British intelligence revealed some important facts about their accountability and responsibility:

Britain has a complicated and rather bureaucratic political control over its intelligence and security community and one that tends to apply itself to long term targets and strategic intelligence program, but has little real influence on the behavior and operations of SIS and MI5. Not so much 'oversight' as blind-sight. Despite the domestic changes of recent years and their formal establishment as legal government organizations, there is still little true accountability for their action or valid test of their overall efficiency. This myriad of organizations include the four main elements of the UK intelligence community; Secret Intelligence Service (MI6) responsible for foreign intelligence, the Security Service (MI5), responsible for internal security and counter espionage within both the UK and Commonwealth countries. The GCHQ, Government Communication Headquarters, SIGINT and COMSEC agency and the DIS, Defense Intelligence Staff, responsible for the intelligence and security activities within the UK armed forces. They report to the JIC and through then to the civil Service (PSIS) and finally the Ministerial Committee (MIS).[2]

However, the issue of interception communication has become more complicated as complaints came from various circles about their privacy and family life. The law of surveillance is be-

---

[1] Established in 1909, MI6 is working as foreign intelligence, responsible to the foreign office of the country. MI6 gathers information overseas.
[2] Britain has a complicated and rather bureaucratic political control over its intelligence and security community and one that tends to apply, *The Guardian*, 26 June 2006

ing amended time and again, but in spite of all these technological efforts, no specific progress has been made in the interception of extremist's e-mails entering the country. The law of terror or the Regulation of Investigatory Power Act 2000 (RIPA), Communication Act 1985 and the Police Act 1997, allow the state security agencies to intercept communications. On 16 June 2013, daily Guardian published a comprehensive report about the role of British intelligence agencies in interception communication which revealed that agencies not only set up fake Internet cafes to secure information on diplomats while RIPA allowed agencies to use all ways of information collection:

> The powers that allow British's intelligence agencies to spy on individuals, including foreign diplomats, were set out in the 1994 Intelligence Services Act (ISA). They were framed in a broad way to allow those involved in espionage to conduct all manner of operations with ministerial authority, and the type of technique used during the G20 summit four years ago suggest a creativity and technological capability The powers that allow Britain's intelligence agencies to spy on individuals, including foreign diplomats, were set out in the 1994 Intelligence Services Act (ISA). They were framed in a broad way to allow those involved in espionage to conduct all manner of operations with ministerial authority, and the types of techniques used during the G20 summit four years ago. After GCHQ, MI5 and MI6 were given their remit through the ISA; the Regulation of Investigatory Powers Act (RIPA) gave the agencies more precise tools to gather intelligence through techniques such as targeted interceptions. Under RIPA, the director general of MI5, the Chief of MI6 and the Director of GCHQ are among 10 very senior officials who can apply for warrant to either the foreign or home secretary.[1]

The interception of communication in the United Kingdom has been central in media and intellectual forums since 2001.

---

[1] *Encyclopedia of Intelligence and Counterintelligence*, Rodney Carlisle, Editor Rodney Carlisle, Routledge, 2015

There have been many complaints in public and government circles regarding the phone tapping, bugging, e-mail hacking and privacy violation, but according to the Regulation of Investigatory Power Act 2000 (RIPA) and, specifically, Interception Communication Act, police and intelligence agencies have legal authority to intercept communication. Orla Lynskey has described the legal control of data sharing with the United States and elucidates the legal aspects of privacy of British citizens in her recent article:

> Following the revelation that US intelligence agencies are engaged in widespread surveillance of internet communications using the so called 'PRISM' program, President Obama's guarantees that PRISM does not apply to US citizens and it does not apply to people living in the US is unlikely to reassure many of this side of the Atlantic. PRISM gives the US National Security Agency (NSA) access to both communications contents and traffic data held of servers of global internet communications heavyweights such as Google, Facebook and Apple. The PRISM revelation quickly led to the concern that the UK's Government Communications Headquarter (GCHQ) was gathering data on UK citizens via PRISM thereby circumventing the protection offered by the UK legal framework. William Hague, appearing before the commons, was quick to refute this claim describing it as 'baseless.'[1]

According to the RIPA's, section 12, Secretary of State can authorize the relevant authority on the issue of interception. However, some people including parliamentarians recorded complaints regarding their telephone monitoring, but there are some laws that allow monitoring the telephone calls. Some laws that authorize state security agencies for monitoring are, Regulation of the Investigatory Power Act 2000 (RIPA), Telecommunications Interception Act of 2000 (TIA), Data Protection Act 1998 (DPA), and Telecommunication Regulations of 1999 (TR).[2]

---

[1] Ibid.
[2] According to the RIPA's, section 12, Secretary of State can authorize the relevant authority on the issue of interception. However, some

In the Annual Report (2012) of the Interception Communications Commissioner, (ICC) presented to Parliament pursuant
to section 58 (6) of the Regulation of Investigatory Power Act
2000, it has been suggested that media and public still needs to
understand RIPA and the way it defines the remit of the commissioner, the Lawful Interception of Communication and the
Acquisition of Communications Data (LICACD). Part-1, Chap-
ter-2 of RIPA provides the power to acquire communications
data. The RIPA bill was introduced in the House of Commons
on 9 February 2000 and completed its parliamentary passage on
26 July.[1]

RIPA regulates the manner in which certain public bodies
may conduct surveillance and access a person's electronic communications. The role of Interception communications Commissioner has been defined in RIPA. Interception and communication has been long established practice in the UK, but before
1985, there was no specific law or framework. Ordinances had
been governing the practice. From 1957 to 1981; government in
the United Kingdom had three official reports available to the
public. These reports were the 1957 Becket Report, the 1980
White Paper and the 1981 Dip lock Report. In 1985, government
hinted about the introduction of Interception Communications
Act. Later on, following the White Paper, the same year, Interception of Communication Act was introduced.[2]

In addition to this, the Government established more joint
intelligence working groups to tackle the issue of terrorism
technically. Joint Terrorism Analysis Centre, Centre for the Protection of National Infrastructure, Joint Intelligence Committee and Assessment Staff and IT centre under the supervision of
GCHQ. All these institutions play very important role in tackling violent extremism and criminal culture in the country. In-

---

people including parliamentarians recorded complaints regarding their
telephone monitoring, but there are some laws that allow monitoring
the telephone calls. Some laws that authorize state security agencies
for monitoring are, Regulation of the Investigatory Power Act 2000
(RIPA), Telecommunications Interception Act of 2000 (TIA), Data
Protection Act 1998 (DPA), and Telecommunication Regulations of
1999 (TR). RIPA *and the Crisis of Britain's Surveillance Sate*, Musa Khan
Jalalzai, 2014
[1] Ibid.
[2] Ibid.

telligence and Security Committee in its report has given much importance to the analysis and responsibilities of the Defense Intelligence Staff (DIS):

> The defense intelligence staffs (DIS) is a critical part of the country intelligence community, and a single largest intelligence analytical capability in the UK." Home Office in its study report has claimed that Internet protocol based communications will render the UK's domestic interception capabilities obsolete over the next decade. However, the Home Secretary told the committee: "We do recognize the changing technology that we are facing, the way in which both the collection and dissemination of information Britain's National Security Challenges and data will change fundamentally, and it will change more quickly in this country then it will in many others...The impact of that will be to massively degrade (unless we make big changes) out ability, not just to be able to intercept, but actually potentially to be able to collect the communications data in the first place in order to be able to target the interception.[1]

Today, citizens of Britain are facing the worst form of cyber terrorism. Cyber warriors use electronic attacks on institutions for many advantages. First, it is cheap and the action is very difficult to trace. Second, they also use the method of distributed denial of services to overburden the government and its agencies' electronic databases. A recent detailed investigation of the Indian government revealed that a cyber spy network operating out of China is targeting Indian business, diplomatic, strategic and academic interests. India complains about Pakistan's cyber attacks as well. However, cyber war between Iran and the Arab world is another interesting story. Iranian hackers have been trying to retrieve sensitive data from the computers of state institutions of various Arab states for years. Meanwhile, aiming to destroy the Iranian nuclear program, Israel sends strong viruses to the computers of Iranian nuclear installations.

The war of intelligence started between European states and

---

[1] Ibid.

the UK when France, Germany and Spain summoned both the UK and US ambassadors to explain the motive behind their surveillance policies. Germany became very angry when it found that the Berlin-based UK embassy was involved in alleged eavesdropping. The revelations by Mr. Snowden sparked widespread outrage not only in Germany but also in other European states. With this, the intelligence war of all Euro-states may possibly start on UK soil as we have already witnessed the arrest of several foreign spies. With the arrival of thousands of European citizens into the UK, the biggest challenge for the British intelligence infrastructure would be to control invisible people, groups and criminal gangs in the streets of its towns and cities. Russia and China have already been identified as having strong espionage networks in the country.

When the Eastern European intelligence networks shifted here, the real game started and it will increase the vulnerability of UK state institutions. A government security document published in The Daily Telegraph warned that the UK is a high priority target for 20 foreign intelligence agencies. Intelligence reports revealed that Iranian, Korean, Serbian and Syrian intelligence agencies have roots in UK society while the intelligence agencies of some European states, such as France and Germany, are also present in the field.

In January 2014, thousands of European citizens started arriving here with new messages, cultures and ways of life. As a small country, the UK is unable to accommodate such a large, unskilled population to provide jobseeker allowances, benefits and housing. Their arrival created a bigger social and security crisis in the country as the incidents of terror-related crimes, theft and benefit fraud have already been exacerbated. History tells us that the EU represents the hostile nations of the first and second world wars, which share poverty, unemployment and homelessness with each other. The MI5 warned that the threat of espionage did not end with the collapse of Soviet communism in the early 1990s. Espionage against UK interests continues and is widespread, insidious and potentially very damaging. The Security Service, on its website, has warned about the vulnerability of institutions to foreign intelligence agencies:

The UK is a high priority espionage target. Many countries actively seek UK information and material to advance their own military, technological, political and economic programs. The activities of intelligence agencies identified as posing the greatest threat are subject to particular scrutiny. The threat against British interests is not confined to within the UK itself. A foreign intelligence service operates best in its own country and therefore finds it easier to target UK interests at home, where they can control the environment and take advantage of any perceived vulnerabilities.[1]

The Sunday Telegraph reported Whitehall's concern about the foreign spying network in the UK. According to the newspaper report, Britain's European neighbors, including Germany and France, were also engaged in industrial and political espionage within the UK. Diplomatic ruction between the UK and other European states over intelligence surveillance has now caused mistrust as they blame each other for spying on their citizens and leaders. The flames of this conflagration are now felt in the UK and can ignite the violent fire of a crucial intelligence war on the country's soil. In this possible war, the UK might face an uneven situation if the European intelligence infrastructure entered into revenge politics. In the near future, this intelligence war may make the UK more vulnerable to hostile secret networks. The police may face an uncontrollable situation in tackling serious organized crime, and intelligence agencies will be in trouble countering unexpected invisible forces.[2]

The UK law enforcement mechanism is in deep crisis as frustration continues to exacerbate the pain of the police department, Home Office and policing intelligence agencies. Metropolitan Police is facing unprecedented difficulty in dealing with criminal gangs, serious organized crime, kidnapping, drug trafficking, illegal immigrants, terrorist networks, extremism and racism across the country, while some research reports highlighted the countrywide operation of foreign sponsored serious organized crime human trafficking networks in conjunction

[1] www.mi5.gov.uk
[2] *The Crisis of Britain's Surveillance Sate*, Musa Khan Jalalzai, 2014.

with spy networks-challenging the authority of law enforce-ment agencies.

One can understand the fear and irritation of our law en-forcement agencies from the fact that terrorist and foreign es-pionage networks across the country are making trouble. They are trying to have access to all networks, but unfortunately, their performance is disappointing. The police department and In November 2012, with the election of police and crime com-missioner election, anti privatization campaign received strong support. Another irksome challenge is that there is less chance for ethnic minority to join the police force. Figure released under the freedom of information act shows that ethnic minorities rep-resent disproportionately low in number. Newly published data shows that 32 of the country 45 territorial police forces appoint a greater number of white people.

In his 1,000 pages report, Mr. Tom maintained that the roots of policing lie in a working class structure, but the ooze needed to be cleared as complaints in the minds of police officers remain unsolved. On 24 July 2012, Police Negotiation Board didn't agree on some proposals relating to pay and conditions, but Mr. Tom Winsor's policing reforms faced strong opposition from some institutions and specific circles. The present pay and condition system were designed 30 years ago which is why Mr. Tom carry out a thorough review to clear the ooze. Terrorist and foreign espionage groups have long tried to attack critical national in-frastructure across the UK but credit goes to the Government Communication Headquarters (GCHQ) for its professional pre-vent measures.[1]

The current war of interests in Ukraine is prompting many problems between Russia and the UK. Britain, which is one of the guarantors of the territorial integrity of Ukraine, is be-ing heavily criticized for its flawed approach to the expanding flare-ups along Europe's borders. In the Euro-committee of the House of Lords, the Cameron administration was deeply criti-

---

[1] On 24 July 2012, the Police Negotiation Board didn't agree on some proposals relating to pay and conditions, but Mr. Tom Winsor's polic-ing reforms faced strong opposition from some institutions and specific circles. The present pay and condition system were designed 30 years ago which is why Mr. Tom carry out a thorough review to clear the ooze. *Daily Times*, 19 January 2016.

cized for a 'catastrophic misreading' of the mood in Russia. Just as the political tension in Ukraine has changed Russian and US priorities, the intelligence war in the UK and the US has also shifted. As a US ally, the UK is facing the challenge of Russian intelligence networks on its soil. Intelligence experts in London say that Russian intelligence efforts have returned to Cold War levels. Interestingly, one of the most important functions performed by British intelligence is to provide timely warnings of hostile intelligence agencies present in the country. In the 1980s and 2000s, MI5 and MI6 were aware of the Russian intelligence networks in Britain.

In 1981, the KGB and the Soviet military intelligence (GRU) had been assigned a special task that included monitoring the workings of 10 Downing Street, the Ministry of Defense, the FCO, the headquarters of the British intelligence agencies and their countrywide contacts with different firms and personalities. In fact, intelligence relations between the UK and Russia have deteriorated since 2006, following the murder of the former KGB agent, Alexander Litvinenko, in London. Alexander Litvinenko was a former FSB officer who arrived in the UK fearing court prosecution. He supported a wanted Russian businessman, Boris Berezovsky, in his media campaign. In 2006, Mr. Litvinenko was poisoned in a hotel and died.[1]

In 2013, when the British Prime Minister visited Moscow, the intelligence agencies of both sides agreed to renew limited cooperation but could not proceed. In July 2007, the Crown Prosecution said that the Russian businessman Boris Berezovsky would not face trial in Britain for talking to the Guardian newspaper about plotting a "revolution" in his homeland. He was wanted in Russia for corruption cases till his death in 2013. In 2008, the Russian government closed the offices of two British Councils.

However, their intelligence relationship turned hostile with the Euro imposition of sanctions against Russia and the UK criticism of the Crimea annexation. In March 2014, Britain suspended all military cooperation with Russia. The most recent incidents of espionage and an intelligence war in Britain are a matter of great concern. These unexpected incidents revolve

---

[1] Ibid.

around foreign espionage networks, an issue that seemingly refused to die out with the end of the Cold War. On January 24, 2015, the FBI charged three men with serving for Russia in New York. These agents, the US newspapers reported, were directed to collect intelligence about the US sanctions against Russia.[1]

With the inception of the new cold war, after the Western-led coup in Ukraine and Crimea's subsequent democratic referendum requesting to leave Ukraine and rejoin Russia (called, by the Western press, "Russia's 'annexation' of Crimea"), the intelligence war between Russia, UK, and the US is being fought in cyberspace.

Britain's powerful intelligence agency (SIS) issued an unprecedented warning that Russian intelligence is targeting British spies and former agents in an aggressive way.[2] According to The Sunday Times report: "A memo was sent to the staff and former employees of the Secret Intelligence Service (SIS) with a warning that Russian agents will undermine their businesses and apply pressure to 'close relations' to gain classified information or recruit double agents."[3]

In Britain, senior policy makers view these initiatives as a policy change towards Russian intelligence operations here. The security service (MI5) directed the counter-espionage branch to step up surveillance against Putin-backed agents on the streets of London. The UK security services begun to recruit a new generation of Russian-speaking spies to help monitor Vladimir Putin's undercover agents as relations worsen between the

---

[1] *The Guardian*, 07 July 2007: The Crown Prosecution said that the Russian businessman Boris Berezovsky would not face trial in Britain for talking to *The Guardian* newspaper about plotting a "revolution" in his homeland. (He was wanted in Russia for corruption cases till his death in 2013. In 2008, the Russian government closed the offices of two British Councils. However, their intelligence relationship turned hostile with the European imposition of sanctions against Russia and the UK's criticism of the return of Crimea to Russia. In March 2014, Britain suspended all military cooperation with Russia.)

[2] Britain's European neighbors, including Germany and France, were also engaged in industrial and political espionage within the UK. Diplomatic ruction between the UK and other European states over intelligence surveillance has now caused mistrust as they blame each other for spying on their citizens and leaders. *Telegraph* 07 February 2009 and *Daily Times*, 07 January 2015.

[3] *Daily Times*, 24 March 2015.

two states. Moreover, Foreign Secretary Philip Hammond also warned that the country's spy agencies were stepping up efforts to counter the FSB and GRU networks. "We are in familiar territory for anyone over the age of about 50 with Russia's aggressive behavior as a stark reminder it has the potential to pose the single greatest threat to our security," Hammond said.[1]

In contrast to the Eye Five Agreement countries, British intelligence is well organized and updated. The changing security environment has also been important in influencing the changing tactics of the UK intelligence agencies. Since 9/11, there has been an increasing amount of literature on how to improve the practice of the intelligence mechanism in the country. Experts suggested that building a better and effective intelligence infrastructure requires getting both the key enabling activities and core intelligence processes. In this regard, the agencies serve a function similar to that of the new media, and the range of information they cover depends on the scope of the nation's intelligence interest. Indeed, the more recent public discussion of intelligence has been characterized by a neglect of fundamental questions about the proper role of intelligence and secrecy in a country. During the last 100 years, British intelligence performed an exceptional role in times of war and peace.

British jihadists, privacy and mass surveillance

As the cauldron is already out of control, extremist users of the internet have put more fuel on the fire. The internet is under close watch by the Tackling Extremism and Radicalization Task Force (TERFOR) to identify terror suspects and jihadist mafia groups in the UK. Since the internet became the main tool and means of communication — and also a source of terrorism — jihadist groups began to invite young people to die in order to kill. In 2014, they have been successful in their mission by sending hundreds of young UK citizens to Iraq, Syria and Islamic State of Iraq and Syria (ISIS) networks in Pakistan and Afghanistan.

Their bomb-making manuals are freely available online and their financing through the internet has become a serious issue. The commissioner of the Metropolitan Police, London, Sir Ber-

---

[1] Ibid.

nard Hogan Howe, recently warned that the internet is becoming a "dark and ungoverned" place for terrorists to safely operate. "Encryption on computers and mobile phones is frustrating police inquiries and leaving parts of the web as 'anarchic places'," Mr. Bernard said. According to a UN report: "The internet may be used not only as a means to publish extremist rhetoric and videos but also a way to develop relationships with, and solicit support from, those most responsive to targeted propaganda."[1]

Though our law enforcement and intelligence agencies are struggling to develop sophisticated tools to prevent detect and deter terrorists' online activities; the issue of mass surveillance in our society has become a headache. We are unable to walk unfettered as mass surveillance has tied our hands and feet, and confined us to a specific domain. From our e-mail box, Facebook profile, Twitter feed and telephone to bedroom, nothing is safe. On 28 October, 2014, Chatham House, an international affairs think tank, organized an event on mass surveillance and counterterrorism, in which UN Special Rapporteur on Counterterrorism and Human Rights Dr Ben Emmerson and Chairman Intelligence and Security Committee of the British Parliament Sir Malcolm Rifkin were the main speakers.

The debate started with the violation of privacy and massive surveillance blankets in the US, Europe and the UK. Dr. Ben Emmerson raised serious questions about the way UK and US surveillance mechanisms operate. The revelations of the new chief of the GCHQ, Robert Hannigan, in his Financial Times article, further complicated the issue when he categorically said that privacy has never been an absolute right. British Foreign Minister Philip Hammond also admitted in his statement before the Parliamentary Intelligence and Security Committee that the bulk data collection did not amount to mass surveillance.[2]

In his public remarks, Mr. Philip said, "Mass surveillance is illegal." In June 2014, the UK's top counterterrorism officials

---

[1] *BBC*, 21 January 2016.
[2] On 28 October, 2014, Chatham House, an international affairs think tank, organized an event on mass surveillance and counterterrorism, in which *UN Special Rapporteur on Counterterrorism and Human Rights* Dr Ben Emmerson and Chairman Intelligence and Security Committee of the British Parliament Sir Malcolm Rifkin were the main speakers. *Daily Times.*

were forced to reveal a secret government policy justifying the mass surveillance of every Facebook, Twitter, and YouTube and Google user in the UK. These revelations were made public due to the deep pressure from Privacy International, Liberty, Amnesty International and the American Civil Liberties Union. Mr. Charles Farr, the director general of the office for security and counterterrorism defended his organization. The bureau of investigative journalism in the UK filed a case with the European Court of Human Rights in Strasbourg, challenging the current UK legislation on mass surveillance and its threat to journalism.[1]

On 29 August, 2014, the UK Prime Minister warned that his country faced the "greatest and deepest" terror threat in history. Mr. David Cameron said that the risk posed by ISIS will last for "decades" and raised the prospect of an expanding terrorist nation "on the shores of the Mediterranean." Privacy and human rights groups complain that these day-to-day changing surveillance mechanisms might possibly alienate citizens from the state. The government and its security infrastructure are also worked up over the exacerbation of prevailing fear of online extremism across the country.[2]

On 01 September, 2014, Prime Minister David Cameron announced a series of new anti-terror measures. In fact, this announcement was the introduction of new powers to be added to the current terror laws. The cyber security strategy of the UK tells us about the challenges of cyber terrorism and the fatality of violent cyber attacks on national computers. Cyber terrorism and attacks on the UK's sensitive computers from a safe distance have become a complex security challenge. Constant connectivity and the way modern cyber terrorism operates have transformed the way individuals, organizations and states interact. Every year, the UK's society is becoming increasingly dependent on information and communications technology. It receives var-

---

[1] Ibid.

[2] On 01 September, 2014, Prime Minister David Cameron announced a series of new anti-terror measures, introducing new powers to be added to the current terror laws. The cyber security strategy of the UK tells us about the challenges of cyber terrorism and the fatality of violent cyber attacks on national computers. Cyber terrorism and attacks on the UK's sensitive computers from a safe distance have become a complex security challenge. Constant connectivity and the way modern cyber terrorism operates have transformed the way individuals, organizations and states interact. *The Guardian*, 01 September 2014.

ious kinds of threats through cyberspace, while our state's computers are being attacked on a daily basis. As the threat of online jihadism exacerbates, the anxiety felt by our government increases. The failure of the government and its frustration are evident from its changing directions and strategies together with the day-to-day introduction of new counterterrorism measures.

New surveillance laws added to the list of UK's mass surveillance have concerned cyber security and law and order experts. They think that these laws might further prompt mistrust between the state and society. Counterterrorism mechanisms by TERFOR and other relevant agencies against the online war on extremism and radicalization is 50-50 or failing as jihadists continue to join ISIS, al Shabab and Boko Haram's ranks in Africa, and Taliban networks in Pakistan and Afghanistan.

We understand that the day-to-day increase in cyber attacks on our computers by Chinese and Russian cyber terrorists are bigger challenges but mass surveillance is not the only way of solving the prevailing jihadist culture in the UK. We have failed to intercept their hate campaign in our streets, mosques and educational institutions. They are intimidating our children openly while intelligence agencies are finding it difficult to control this hydra. The GCHQ continues to store their emails, data, text messages and images but the result is still poor. Finally, we are still working to prepare our horses for the long and tenacious battle ahead and request professionals to join our intelligence war against terrorism and radicalization.

The taskforce (TERFOR) sets out the government's aim of tackling all forms of extremism, but recognizes that the greatest risk to the security of the UK comes from Al Qaeda and like-minded groups. The report gives the definition of "extremism" used in the 2011 'Prevent' Strategy. It also provides a definition of "Islamist extremism," which should not be confused with traditional religious practice. Challenging extremism is a shared effort for both government and communities in the UK.

The report sets out practical proposals to tackle extremism in the following areas:

1. Disrupting extremists
2. Countering extremist narratives and ideology
3. Preventing radicalization
4. Integration

(The Prime Minister set up the Extremism Task Force to identify any areas where our current approach was lacking and to agree practical steps to fight against all forms of extremism. 4 December 2013, Cabinet Office 70 Whitehall, https://www.gov.uk/government/uploads/system/uploads/attachment_data/file/263181/ETF_FINAL.)

Chapter 9. Cyber Terrorism and Security Challenges of the United Kingdom

In newspapers, journals, social and electronic media, the quizzical statements of the British government about the vulnerability and insecurity of the country's population and national critical infrastructure have created an impression that the UK is no longer a secure business and investment environment. Every month, newspapers publish lurid statements of law-enforcement commanders about the prevailing extremist and terror culture across the country, in which they consecutively demand more funds to effectively counter it, but in reality, it is not clear how terrorism and extremism is being fought. We have about 85 terrorist networks operating across the country with its well-trained professional army, but counter terrorism authorities and police commanders say they know little about all these terror nests.

This drumbeating about the intensifying terror threat has now become an old mantra, but it is clear that the threat to national security is very much real. Sectarianism, racism and discrimination are there, and the wave of targeted killings has become more violent. Every day innocent citizens are targeted in streets, markets and towns, but the police are helpless to tackle the issue with an iron hand.

The threat of terrorism and extremism are elevated due to

the nation's military engagement in South Asia and the Middle East. As we experienced on November 20, 2012, law enforcement agencies carried out a large pre-planned intelligence-led operation against terror suspects and arrested only a few people to update their records. The British law-enforcement and intelligence also face an invisible threat of cyber terrorism. Cyber warriors and hackers from across the border attack computers of various government institutions.

During the last two decades, cyber terrorists have attacked thousands of websites including the websites of the UK government, causing millions of pounds in damage. Now this war has reached a breaking point. To combat the forces of financial jihad, Britain's Cyber Security Strategy was published in November 2011, which underlined the technicality of the threat faced by the country's institutions from economic jihadists and state-sponsored cyber forces. The basic objectives of the UK Cyber Security Strategy are to introduce the traditions of partnership and transparency both across business and within the international community in an effort to meet the growing cyber threat.

The Security Service (MI5) recently warned that cyber crime, espionage and cyber terrorism pose a major threat to the national security of the country. The issue has been the focus of international media for a decade while the British government seems to have failed in intercepting the invasion of Chinese cyber warriors. We have been told in the past that intelligence agencies play an important part in helping to tackle the threat of economic warfare, but numerous complaints from various state institutions, including defense and foreign ministries, indicate that the campaign against information warfare has been less effective in the past.

All strategies and plans of government and its institutions have failed to respond to the cyber espionage and attacks of China, India and North Korea. Experts see cyber crime as an unauthorized network that breaches data. A cyber attack on Sony Entertainment and on sensitive computers in the UK and US took place 24 November 2014, illustrating how hard it is to categorize attacks and formulate appropriate responses. Cyber warriors disabled all the information technology system of the Sony Entertainment. State and private institutions have already been experiencing cyber attacks against their websites for a decade, and in the meantime new groups of financial jihadists have been training hackers to wage war against the global financial markets. These are skilled, educated experts in cyber warfare, and they have the capability to destroy and disrupt any financial network around the world. They can hack into the servers of state institutions and private companies, and use those servers, without being discovered.

The UK specified four objectives in 2011 geared to shoring up cyber security and "protecting and promoting the UK in a digital world. These objectives are spelled out in the next several pages. However, if we study these four objectives in detail, we may find that the government remains quite unable to fight cyber terrorism despite all the rhetoric.

Economic warriors and cyber terrorists launch hundreds of thousands of attacks across the world every day and collect important military and financial data from various government and private institutions. E-Warriors use cyberspace to facilitate their attacks, and use websites to spread messages and recruit supporters around the world. In the near future, cyber terrorism and economic jihad will be able to target all Britain state institutions as the Internet has been a driving force behind the modernization of the world's economy and military industry. Terrorists may use computers not only to inflict damage to the security infrastructure but to disrupt the whole communication system. Former director GCHQ, Professor Sir David Omand suggested: "Maintaining community confidence in the action of the state is important. Good pre-emptive intelligence can reassure the community by removing the extremists and by disrupting any potential attack without having to fall back on the sort of blunt discriminatory measures that alienate moderate support within the community on which effective policing and counter terrorism depends."

Government and law enforcement agencies are increasingly concerned about the possible cyber attack from extremist groups, foreign hackers and intelligence networks with malicious intent, such as terrorism and acts of disruption. The Chief of GCHQ has warned about the cyber threat to UK security and economic security in particular. Mr. Loban warned that the country is witnessing the development of criminal market place, where cyber dollars are traded in exchange for a citizen's credit cards details. In the present global marketplace, the Internet is no longer just about e-mail and websites. This machine empowers the growing list of revenue-generating e-business activities. But in the near future, cyber terrorism and economic jihad can target all Britain state institutions.

The Internet is emerging as a security threat to all nations across the globe as terrorists easily communicate through Internet and receive instructions for attacks. The Internet is widely regarded as a center of information, a bigger library, an asset of literature and unfortunately a hub for many violent things. In these circumstances, both the US and UK have introduced strict surveillance measures to tackle the threats emanating from Internet or online activities. Chancellor George Osborne recently suggested that MI5 and MI6 must concentrate on cyber terrorism and devote more money and manpower defending Britain from the cyber attacks of hostile states.

In 2011, diplomatic ruction between the US and China over the establishment of North Korea's cyber army (180,000 cyber warriors) became the central issue when the US State Department accused Pyongyang of developing a cyber force capable of destroying vital infrastructure and military data of other states. The US Secretary of State termed this development as the largest single security threat to the country's interests. Some recent reports allege that China has developed a strong cyber army and e-espionage networks around the world to collect important financial and military data from private and state institutions. An FBI report alleged the number of Chinese cyber intelligence and spy networks of being over 30,000 plus 150,000 spies.

In a London Conference on Cyberspace, experts agreed on the point that the threat to information security in the UK and Europe intensified as skilled and trained hackers from several states managed to wage economic jihad against the state and private institutions. In his speech, former British Foreign Secretary William Hague issued a stern warning to countries involved in financial terrorism against other states and said this undeclared war is unacceptable. Prime Minister David Cameron warned that this warfare is against Britain's interests.

The threat of cyber terrorism has generated panic across the globe, specifically in the United Kingdom as cyber terrorists continues to target the state owned computer systems. In newspapers, journals and in books, researchers warned that the UK financial markets, banking sectors, and national critical infrastructure are under threat from cyber terrorists representing various nationalities. Over the last decades, several competent technologies have developed that pose serious threat to states and private institutions. With the emergence of these technologies and several definitions of cyber terrorism, many unknown terms also appeared in the pages of books and newspapers. These terms in the cyber domain confused experts and common people to grasp the true concept and definition of cyber terrorism.[1]

In 2011, Chatham House, a UK based think tank, published a detailed report on the evolving threat of cyber terrorism to the country critical national infrastructure. Its researchers asked different question in their survey to find out how this menace needed to be tackled. In this report, they have also highlighted the legal aspects and counter measures:

> The United Kingdom National Security Strategy (NNS), and Strategic Defense and Security review (SDSR) released in October 2010 promoted cyber security to a Tier One risk to national security, and its high status was reinforced by the UK government's allocation of £650 million to cyber security and intelligence. The UK Ministry of Defense's December 2010 Green Paper entitled "Equipment, Support and Technology for UK Defense and Security noted that perhaps the over-riding characteristics of cyberspace are the space of change.[2]

---

[1] Innovation and the UK's knowledge economy, Department of Business & skills, The RT Hon Dr Vince Cable speech in parliament, 22 July 2014, https://www.gov.uk/government/speeches/innovation-and-the-uks-knowledge-economy

[2] Cyber security and the UK's critical national infrastructure, Paul Cornish, David Livingston, Dave Clemente and Claire Yorker, A Chatham House report, 2011, also *Business and Technology Magazine*, November 2012.

On 02 April 2016, Prime Minister David Cameron warned that the ISIS may possibly use drones to spray nuclear materials over western cities. Telegraph reported that there was growing concerns among world leaders that extremists are looking to buy commercial drones to launch a dirty bomb attack over major metropolitan cities, which could kill thousands. US officials reportedly fear that extremists could steal radioactive material from a medical facility and sold through the "dark web." Prime Minister Cameron said Britain would deploy counterterrorism police and the UK Border Force while British leaders held a Cobra meeting. Mr. Cameron said at the summit that Britain planed to hire 1,000 more armed police and deploy counterterrorism units in cities outside London to help counter any possible attack.

The UK Defense Secretary wowed that his country would spend £40 million on a new cyber security centre designed to protect Ministry of Defense networks and systems from "malicious actors," "Britain is a world leader in cyber security but with growing threats this new operations centre will ensure that our armed forces continue to operate securely," Fallon said. The UK think tank Privacy International (PI) called on the government to use targeted surveillance to tackle threats from terrorists and organized criminals rather than collecting people's private online data. The UK and United States will take part in a joint exercise.[1]

The attacks in Brussels raised fresh concerns about the prospect of nuclear terrorism, with fears Islamic State militants may attempt to get hold of materials to create a 'dirty bomb'. But the cyber attack exercise with the US would ensure that both governments and their civil nuclear industries were prepared and could address any potential weaknesses. The Prime Minister said terrorists would "like to kill as many people as they possibly could" amid fears Islamic State jihadists could attempt to create a dirty bomb. The UK and United States will take part in a joint exercise next year to prepare for any online attack against

---

[1] Policy paper 2010–2015, Cyber Security 08 May 2015, 3-Policy paper, 2010 to 2015 government policy: cyber security, 8 May 2015, https://www.gov.uk/government/publications/2010-to-2015-government-policy-cyber-security/2010-to-2015-government-policy-cyber-security.

nuclear power plants and waste storage facilities. Cyber attacks and high-profile data breaches are the biggest threat to business in 2016, according to a survey of 500 companies from around the world. The number of companies expressing fear over the potential loss of sensitive data has also increased from 74% to 80%.[1]

The threat of Cyber Terrorism has intensified

The government tried to bring its multitudinous powers together in a single bill. In this it has failed, with a number of important powers still lying outside the scope of the checks and oversights proposed under the draft legislation. "The entire surveillance system in the UK desperately needs dragging out of the shadows and into the light of day. On 01 July 2015 the Investigatory Powers Tribunal (IPT) –notified Amnesty International that UK government agencies had spied on the organization by intercepting, accessing and storing its communications.

The GCHQ was once censured for not revealing enough about how it shares information with its American counterparts. The Investigatory Powers Tribunal said GCHQ failed until December 2014 to make clear enough details of how it shared data from mass internet surveillance. In its disclosures in December, the GCHQ said UK intelligence services were "permitted" to request information gathered by Prism and Upstream-US surveillance systems which can collect information on "non-US persons." However, the legal framework governing the intrusive capabilities of intelligence agencies is unnecessarily complicated and – crucially – lacks transparency, it said, and it called for the current legislation to be replaced by a new, single act of parliament.[2]

A new industry of information theft developed across the globe now sends its trained members to developed nations to steal their sensitive financial and industrial data. They are not tanks and truck bombs; they are missiles who target the institutional assets of various states from safe distances. As western societies have now become completely dependent on information technologies, attacks on their computers have increased;

[1] The United States Department of State, http://www.state.gov/j/ct/info/c16718.htm.

[2] *Journal of information technology education, Volume-3,* 2004, Lynn Hunt.

cyber terrorists steal personal data and trade secrets and crackers break into their computer systems. These acts of terrorism caused severe economic loss and damage in the United Kingdom. The activities of these cyber terror networks are greatly enhanced by the use of the Internet that undermines distances and geographical boundaries.

Recent reports in newspapers have quoted President Obama as saying that the cyber threat is one of the most serious economic and national security challenges. In July 2012, the director of the US National Security Agency (NSA) labeled cyber espionage the cause of the greatest transfer of wealth in history, citing data on cyber attacks against US companies that have siphoned off vast quantities of intellectual property and industrial information. Britain is an easy target of cyber terrorism as various institutions recently reported the vulnerability of their computer data.

The lack of an international agreement among states on cyber terrorism is thwarting efforts to bring hackers to justice, according to the UNODC report. The report's focus is cyber warfare; cyber groups and young hackers use the internet for terrorist purposes. They distribute propaganda to incite violence: "Governments need to work together to stop cyber attacks and operating systems must be redesigned," Eugen Kaspersky, the founder of Kaspersky Lab, warned. Kaspersky, whose lab discovered the flame virus that has attacked computers in Iran, told reporters in Tel Aviv University: "It's not cyber war, it's cyber terrorism; and I'm afraid it's just the beginning of the game . . . I'm afraid it will be the end of the world as we know it."[1]

Under this program, GCHQ, MI5, NSA and FBI would try to improve information sharing process, cooperate with each other and fight cyber terrorism with competency. However, there were speculations that the Islamic State (ISIS) may carryout cyber attack to kill many people in Britain. Daily Mail reported George Osborne as saying that: "ISIS could kill British citizens by launching cyber attacks on hospitals and air traffic control, Osborne warned. In his speech at the headquarters of GCHQ, Osborne said that if ISIS attacked, it will disrupt all government

---

[1] *Response to cyber terrorism, Centre of excellence*, Ankara, Turkey, March 2008, http://www.iospress.nl/book/responses-to-cyber-terrorism.

systems including, hospitals, and satellite and air traffic control," Osborne warned.[1]

On 14 July 2014, Britain allocated £1.1 billion for defense to fight cyber terrorism. David Cameron ordered armed forces to fight the unseen enemy. "Britain military must be enhanced to defeat against the threat of terrorist attacks as well as the potential for extra immigration if "fragile and lawless state fracture," Mr. Cameron warned. In my previous article, I warned that there are cyber networks operating in the country with the ability to acquire invisible quantities of sensitive data of various state institutions. These networks might be linked to some states. China, Russia, India and North Korea are cyber superpowers and possess technological know how to manage successful attacks from a safe distance.[2]

These countries have trained thousands of cyber warriors for cyber attacks on the institutional networks of other states and establish strong economic espionage networks. The US and UK have failed to meet these challenges. In the UK, the GCHQ changed its strategy by establishing an academic research institute in partnership with the global uncertainties program of the Research Councils' (RCUK) and the Department of Business Innovation and Skills. This newly established institute to counter the cyber aggression of China in Britain is still in the process of improvement. Whitehall is in frustration what to do and how to respond to the growing fear of cyber terrorism. Intelligence agencies demand a £ 2. 1 billion budget for 2014-15. In 2014, government announced a £ 650 million strategy to protect the country from cyber terrorism, because the GCHQ reported that cyber attacks targeting sensitive data in government institutions reached disturbing level.

Chancellor George Osborne suggested that MI5 and MI6 need to concentrate on cyber terrorism and devote more money and manpower to defending Britain from the cyber attacks of hostile powers. However, the case is different here as the intel-

---

[1] "Britain joins US war on Islamist cyber terrorism," *Huffington Post*, 16 January 2015.
[2] ISIS plot to use cyber jihadists to bring down airlines and target UK nuclear power stations and hospitals, 17 November 2015, www.dailymail.co.uk/isis.

ligence and security committee last year warned that much of the task to secure the country's networks in cyberspace is still at an early stage. The Foreign Secretary warned that organized attacks on a daily basis against government networks are more irksome. On September 6, 2012, he launched a government guide to cyber security for business. The UK has developed weapons to counter the threat from hackers, William Hague said.[1]

On 17 November 2015, George Osborne decided to double the budget to finance fight against cyber terrorism while refusing to confirm that budget cut to be announced soon. The United Kingdom had to spend £1.9 billion over five year countering ISIS and its use of Internet to plane attack against the government installations. In his GCHQ office speech, Mr. Osborne said GCHQ offensive capabilities to counter ISIS would be improved. The GCHQ was told to work with the Defense Ministry to develop countering techniques against the ISIS use of Internet. Britain intelligence agencies have limited man power. Only 12,700 people are not sufficient force to fight the ISIS, but they are competent.[2]

Saying that the world is more vulnerable than the last five years, on 23 November 2015, Prime Minister David Cameron presented Britain's National Security Strategy and Strategic Defense and Security Review (SDSR) in Parliament. The United Kingdom has been experiencing cyber attacks on state computers for a decade. Cyber warriors continue to attack private sectors as well.[3]

Snowden's leaks implicated Britain's signals intelligence agency, GCHQ, pretty much immediately after a Guardian story focused on its access to material collected via the then-classified PRISM program. Other revelations quickly followed, such as GCHQ's ability to attach intercept probes to fiber-optic cables carrying internet and phone traffic; its development of specific internet buffers, enabling it to store this data (Operation TEMPORA); and its ability to intercept and store webcam images (Operation Optic Nerve). The legislation which immediately

---

[1] David Cameron pledges £1.1 billion for defense to fight cyber terrorists, *Telegraph*, 14 July 2014.
[2] *The Independent*, 6 June 2014.
[3] Terror threat: UK power stations at risk from deadly nuclear attack, *Daily Express*, 17 November 2015.

came under examination was the Regulation of Investigatory Powers Act (RIPA) 2000, the legal framework that underpins the government's interception of communications. RIPA has long been regarded as overly complex, confusing, and dense.

The four objectives of the UK cyber security strategy

In a nutshell, here is the "UK Cyber Security Strategy: Protecting and promoting the UK in a digital world."[1]

Objective 1: Tackling cyber crime and making the UK one of the most secure places in the world to do business in cyberspace.

Objective 2: Making the UK more resilient to cyber attack and better able to protect our interests in cyberspace.

Objective 3: Helping to shape an open, vibrant and stable cyberspace which the UK public can use safely and that supports open societies.

Objective 4: Building the UK's cross-cutting knowledge, skills and capability to underpin all our cyber security objectives.

Additionally, the draft of Investigatory Powers Bill[2] addresses issues of fundamental importance for the country's security.

1. The Investigatory Power Bill features changes to make sure that UK law is brought in line with European law, following the adoption of a directive relating to cyber security in August 2013.

2. The Investigatory Powers Bill overhauls the framework governing the use of surveillance by the intelligence and security agencies and law enforcement to obtain the content of communications and communications data

3. Online safety: Content filtering by UK Internet Service Providers (ISPs)

4. Internet surveillance Law

5. Interception communication law

6. Protection from Harassment Act 1997

7. Criminal Justice and Public Order Act 1994

[1]https://www.gov.uk/government/uploads/system/uploads/attachment_data/file/60961/uk-cyber-security-strategy-final.pdf.
[2] National Crime Agency website.

8. Malicious Communications Act 1988
9. Communications Act 2003
10. Breach of the Peace (Scotland)
11. Defamation Act 2013

The National Cyber Crime Unit

1. The NCCU leads the UK's response to cyber crime, supports partners with specialist capabilities and coordinates the national response to the most serious of cyber crime threats.

2. Working closely with the Regional Organized Crime Units (ROCUs), the MPCCU (Metropolitan Police Cyber Crime Unit), and partners within Industry, Government and International Law Enforcement, the NCCU has the capability to respond rapidly to changing threats. "Cyber crime is one of the most significant criminal threats to the UK. The NCA is helping to build the capacity of its partners across the country and coordinating the UK's collective efforts as part of the response." —Andy Archibald, NCCU Deputy Director

3. The NCCU has the capability to respond in fast time to rapidly changing threats and collaborates with partners to reduce cyber crime by:

4. Providing a powerful and highly visible investigative response to the most serious incidents of cyber crime: pursuing cyber criminals at a national and international level.

5. Working proactively to target criminal vulnerabilities and prevent criminal opportunities

6. Assisting the NCA and wider law enforcement to pursue those who utilize the internet or ICT for criminal means. This includes offering technical, strategic and intelligence support to local and regional law enforcement, as well as supporting the training of the Cyber Crime Units within each ROCU.

7. Driving a step-change in the UK's overall capability to tackle cyber crime, supporting partners in industry and law enforcement to better protect themselves against cyber crime, (National Crime Agency website).

CHAPTER 10. FROM THE COLD WAR TO THE CODE WAR

Research reports and official warnings of the UK government about the intensifying threat of cyber terrorism in the print and electronic media prompted torment and cheerlessness in investment and business firms across the country. Cyber security organizations are desperately seeking ways to counter it effectively while private business firms are looking towards the most trusted intelligence agency, the Government Communication Headquarters (GCHQ) for an improvised action against the clandestine networks of hackers and cyber jihadists. As we are being told about the sensitivity of this violent security threat, our intelligence agencies are also restive and anxious about the day-to-day changing mechanism of cyber terrorist groups. The recent violent attacks on the Home Office, Foreign Office, private industry and market economy forced the GCHQ to request cyber technology experts for help in preventing these exacerbating attacks.[1]

The country's Emergency Response Team (ERT) is in hot water as it failed to respond positively. As part of a £ 650 million government investment in countering cyber terrorism, the unit has the core responsibility to respond to the looming threat

---

[1] *BBC News,* 01 April 2016.

of economic jihadists more effectively. Officials in their statements warned government and private firms time and again that Russian, Chinese, Indian and North Korean cyber armies use modern technologies to steal important data. The Cameron government spent billions of pounds to counter cyber armies in a professional way but there was no specific achievement to tell the nation that our agencies are competent to win the battle.[1]

Government agencies are being attacked up to 33,000 times a month by cyber terrorist networks. For public gratification, the GCHQ told the media that the agency was struggling to recruit more people into the cyber security field while the country is at risk of being "left behind and at a disadvantage globally." The UK asks why, as a member state of the Eye-Five intelligence alliance which has developed the strongest surveillance mechanisms, it has failed to respond to this violent threat effectively? Every year, the Cameron government has highlighted cyber terrorism as one of its priorities alongside international terrorism, but its forces still needed modern technology. When the crisis deepened, Prime Minister David Cameron announced a £1.1 billion investment in a military program to tackle these modern threats.[2]

This money was mostly used to pay for new hi-tech surveillance and intelligence gathering equipment. However, the head of counter terrorism in the Metropolitan Police Department, Mark Rowley, appealed to the public for help in identifying jihadist terrorists in communities. Terror-related incidents have increased fivefold. "The growth of dangerous individuals poses challenges for policing, especially when nearly half of Syria travelers of concern were not known as terrorist risks previously," Rowley revealed. In 2013, NATO responded to this economic jihad in the case of the Cooperative Cyber Defense Centre for Excellence and published a 330-page report that prompted reaction from Russia. The document was called 'Tallinn Manual of Cyber Warfare.' The manual's biggest section is devoted to

---

[1] On 19 November 2015, the French Prime Minister, Manuel Valls, raised the specter of ISIS planning a chemical or biological attack, *Daily Telegraph* London.
[2] *The Guardian* 25 March 2016.

cyber attacks that accompany traditional armed conflicts.[1]

In March 2014, NATO and its allies experienced cyber attacks on a large scale while the Syrian Electronic Army (SEA) announced on Twitter that it had successfully hacked into the networks of CENTCOM that oversees US military operations from Turkey to Afghanistan as well as Pacific Command. In Afghanistan, underground cyber strategic commands have established strong networks and retrieve the US, NATO, UK and ISAF's military and operational plans through their cyber warriors easily. They have trained their partners who work for them and purvey top secret military and intelligence information to their cyber commands.[2]

The attacks of Chinese and Russian cyber commandos on NATO computers and the leakage of their military secrets have raised serious questions. As the cyber war has intensified in Asia and Europe, Russia, China and India have started relying on cyber hackers to dig into the UK and US data goldmines. They spend billions of dollars on modernizing their cyber armies every year. Recently, the GCHQ launched an online game in a bid to find the cyber defense talent of the future, but using games to identify a future computer whiz cannot help our agencies if they are still weak in strategy and recruitment.

By 2017, the defense Ministry of Russia plans to complete the formation of a special cyber security force designed to protect its armed forces' networks. This plan is part of a wider program to modernize its information security. A report from Moscow also revealed that Russian military forces are planning to begin setting up cyber warfare forces for both defense and cyber attacks. The force will be headed by an army general. Russian media continues to publish news stories about the digitization of the country's armed forces to compete with US and NATO allies' forces in Asia and Europe. The need for a cyber defense shield has been prompted by the armed forces' transition to new types of weapons with a high share of digital components.[3]

---

[1] Within the framework of these instruments and the IAEA activities and program, Pakistan is committed to international cooperation consistent with our national priorities, *Dawn*, 02 April 2016.

[2] *The Guardian* 25 March 2016.

[3] The CBRN System, "Assessing the threat of terrorist use of chemical, biological, radiological and nuclear weapons in the United Kingdom."

Many of the details remain unknown, but according to recent reports in the Russian media, this defense force will have different levels of technical, cryptographic and radio-electronic security duplicating each other and protecting strategic defense facilities. The UK government was planning to spend more funds on its cyber defense as a recent report has warned about possible cyber attacks on national critical infrastructure. The Prime Minister is committed to spending more money on intelligence and surveillance equipment that includes cyber defense technology. Terrorism in cyber space is increasingly considered as one of the most violent acts against the country's financial sectors. Cyber warfare is an increasing threat to investment and business communities in the UK.

The Crisis of Surveillance and Security

The UK has played an important political and military role in major international conflicts. During the 20th century, the country redefined its place in world politics, and commanded a worldwide empire as a powerful state. After 9/11, the decline of its economy and social stratification generated numerous challenges. The country now is in deep social and economic crisis. Its welfare state is going to shrink and shatter as mafia groups develop networks of criminal trade and a containerized market economy. During the last 50 years, public debt rose. Interest rates are at a nadir. Welfare bills amount to 1.4 trillion pounds. Benefit spending has also doubled over the past decade and reached 157 billion pounds. In March 2014, a large number of parliamentarians voted in favor of benefit caps but no improvement occurred. This decision caused many social problems.[1]

Economic expert Anthony B Atkinson says, "The current rules for benefit eligibility have proved politically toxic, and there is considerable unease about the rules applied to people living in a country but not being domiciled for tax purposes."

An International Security Programme Report, Paul Cornish, Chatham House, February 2007.
[1] On 01 April 2016, *Telegraph* reported that the British Prime Minister warned that ISIS was planning to use drones to spray nuclear materials over Western cities. A British official told newspapers that world leaders have already seen the Islamic State is trying to obtain nuclear, chemical and biological weapons.

There are over one million illegal immigrants across the country that work day and night but do not pay taxes. However, the working class is in trouble managing their day-to-day expenditures and the low wages way of life traps many people in tax credits. More than two and a half million people have been out of work for years. According to some reports, rising numbers of social housing tenants have been trapped badly by recent social reforms. Poor mothers facing deep financial crisis and their children have been reduced to the level of malnutrition. In Scotland, according to the Child Poverty Action report, numerous children face poverty in the near future.[1]

According to a Daily Mail special report, National Health Service (NHS) hospitals kill more than 130,000 patients every year. General practitioners (GPs) behave like Afghan warlords in their clinics. According to a recent report, more than three million patients failed to book their appointment with GPs. Meanwhile, the UK welfare state faces evolving threats from many quarters, like corruption within the police department, domestic radicalization, increasing homelessness and the NHS — where doctors are prematurely ending the lives of thousands of elderly patients via the deadly "Liverpool Care Pathway." Citizens feel insecure amidst the prevailing criminal and violent culture across the country. European and Asian criminal gangs have a free hand to challenge the power of the police and threaten business communities. Numerous shops are looted every day. Intellectuals, writers, professors, experts and professionals continue to leave the country for Australia, Canada, the US, New Zealand and Europe due to the difficulties they face.[2]

On 30 July 2015, Daily Mail London reported the killing of

---

[1] On 18 September 2015, Rose Gottemoeller, the US Under Secretary for Arms Control and International Security in a nuclear security conference, The Citadel's Intelligence and Security Conference "Achieving a Higher Degree of National Security," warned that nuclear materials are falling into the hands of terrorists, Rose Gottemoeller, Under Secretary Remarks in Arms Control and International Security, "The Citadel's Intelligence and Security Conference "Achieving a Higher Degree of National Security", Charleston, South Carolina, September 18, 2015, The US Department of State.
[2] Senior research fellow at the Centre for European Reform Hugo Brady in his research paper (Intelligence, emergencies and foreign policy: The EU's role in counter-terrorism) analyzed the weakness and incompetency of EU policing and intelligence agencies.

innocent people by the NHS staff through Liverpool Pathway Care. The Liverpool Care Pathway, the newspaper reported caused NHS staff to take an "industrialized approach" to the treatment of dying patients, a leading doctor admitted. Professor Rob George, president of the Association of Palliative Medicine, told the Mail how medical staff became obsessed with "ticking the boxes" rather than basic human compassion. He was speaking as the NHS watchdog the National Institute for Health and Care Excellence (NICE) published new guidelines to finally replace the pathway. The controversial pathway, under which fluid and foods are withdrawn from dying patients, was officially abolished by hospitals last year following concerns raised by the Mail that it was causing harrowing suffering.[1]

Despite this, nurses, academics and cancer charities say it is still being used by some staff under a different name. The pathway, Mail reported, was introduced in the Nineties, but the review by Baroness Neuberger in 2013 called for hospitals to phase it out over the subsequent 12 months. Tony Bonser, whose 35-year-old son Neil was put on the pathway four years ago when he was dying from cancer, said families were routinely kept in the dark. "The problems arose because of a lack of communication — we, as his parents, didn't know what was going on," he said. "No one was telling us that he was terminally ill and the word dying was never used. Towards the end of his life we were totally unaware that death was approaching, and so when it did happen it was a shock."[2]

They are calling for an independent regulator to be appointed with investigatory and disciplinary powers to examine serious incidents in the NHS. In 2014, the Royal College of Surgeons warned that elderly people are being denied life-saving operations because of age discrimination within the NHS. It is illegal to discriminate against elderly people, but charities say it still happens. Data released for the first time showed that across large areas of the country, almost no patients above the age of 75 are receiving surgery for breast cancer or routine operations

---

[1] *Daily Mail*, London, 30 July 2015.
[2] "How Mail killed death pathway: Box-ticking NHS staff turned killing patients into an industry, says top doctor," Sophie Borland. *Daily Mail* London, 29 Jul 2015).

such as gall bladder removal and knee replacements.[1]

In 2013, Daily Mail reported the Government introduced age discrimination laws which mean patients should not be denied procedures on grounds of age. Doctors are supposed to assess patients based on their fitness for an operation, and likely benefit from it. Elderly patients are confronted with widespread and systematic inadequate care during their stay, which is a significant problem affecting the vast majority of hospitals in England, it says. Daily Mail also reported the daughter of a pensioner who died of pneumonia after waiting five hours for an ambulance and another 14 in a London A&E today blamed the worst NHS "crisis" in a decade for her mother's death. Helen Forde waited in agony as she watched Bridget Forde, 92, drift in and out of consciousness after falling and breaking her hip. Frantic for help, she dialed 999 for her mother four times, the newspaper reported.[2]

Daily Mail (December 2015) reported hundreds of patients die every year after emergency surgery because there are not enough nurses to care for them, research suggests. A five-year investigation into death rates in English NHS hospitals found those with the highest staffing levels had the lowest death rates. Experts who analyzed the chance of dying within 30 days of being admitted for an emergency operation discovered a five-fold variation in death rates across 156 NHS hospital trusts – from 1.6% at the best trust to 8% at the worst. Crucially, the hospitals with the worst survival records had far fewer nurses, doctors and surgeons. When the hospital trusts were divided into the best, middle and worst groups in terms of the number of nurses and doctors per patient — researchers linked a 7% difference in death rates to staffing alone, the newspaper reported.[3]

A serial killer nurse within the notorious NHS organization named Chua was found "guilty of two murders and poisoning 20 other patients on NHS wards, he used to inject insulin into saline to kill Tracey Arden and Derek Weaver, and he either ad-

---

[1] BBC 09 January 2015.

[2] Ibid.

[3] *Daily Mail* (December 2015) reported hundreds of patients die every year after emergency surgery because there are not enough nurses to care for them, research suggests. A five-year investigation into death rates in English NHS hospitals found those with the highest staffing levels had the lowest death rates.

ministered poison himself or left them for colleagues to use. The Police believed Filipino father-of-two may have faked his qualifications. After 11 days of deliberations, jury convicted him of 34 of 37 charges.[1]

What is the license to kill (The Liverpool Care Pathway or LCP) for the Dying Patient, a UK care pathway? It was developed to help doctors and nurses provide quality end-of-life care.

The Liverpool Care Pathway was developed by Royal Liverpool University Hospital and Liverpool's Marie Curie Hospice in the late 1990s for the care of terminally ill cancer patients. The LCP was then extended to include all patients deemed dying. Daily Telegraph (2012) reported that the LCP continued to be controversial. Many witnesses have testified that elderly patients were admitted to hospital for emergency treatment and put on the LCP without documented proof that the patient consented to it, or could not recover from their health problem. On 15 July 2015 the Guardian reported that more than a million over-65s a year are treated poorly while in hospital, for example by not being helped to eat. Elderly patients are confronted with widespread and systematic inadequate care during their stay, which is a significant problem affecting the vast majority of hospitals in England, it says, the newspaper reported.[2]

On 19 June 2012, Daily Mail reported an eminent British doctor told a meeting of the Royal Society of Medicine in London that every year 130,000 elderly patients who die while under the care of the National Health Service (NHS) have been effectively euthanized by being put on the controversial Liverpool Care Pathway (LCP), a protocol for care of the terminally ill that he described as a "death pathway." Dr. Patrick Pullicino, a consultant neurologist for East Kent Hospitals and Professor of Clinical Neurosciences at the University of Kent, claimed that doctors are putting people on the LCP without proper analysis

---

[1] On 18 May 2015, *Daily Mail.*

[2] *Daily Telegraph* (2012) reported that the LCP continued to be controversial. Many witnesses have testified that elderly patients were admitted to hospital for emergency treatment and put on the LCP without documented proof that the patient consented to it or could not recover from their health problem. On 15 July 2015 *The Guardian* reported that each year more than a million over-65-year-olds are treated poorly while in hospital, for example by not being helped to eat.

of their condition, citing "pressure on beds and difficulty with nursing confused or difficult-to-manage elderly patients" as factors. According to the Daily Mail report, the doctor sounded the alarm that of the approximately half million deaths in Britain each year of elderly people who are in hospital or under NHS care, about 29%, or 130,000, are patients who were on the LCP.[1]

Due to the changing security environment and deteriorating law and order situation, law enforcement agencies have failed to control the mafia of 3,000 criminal gangs. The threat of terrorism is there and the fight against extremists continues but there are more than 90,000 criminals selling narcotics on the streets and in schools and colleges of the country. The overwhelming picture of intrusion into people's personal lives has caused a breakdown in trust between the citizens and the state. Five Eyes (the intelligence alliance between Britain, the US, Australia, Canada and New Zealand), TEMPORA, PRISM, ECHELON and the politics of the intelligence war in cyberspace have shaken the public perception that their governments respect civil rights and liberties.

The revelations of Edward Snowden also sparked widespread outrage about illegal NSA surveillance mechanisms. The intelligence war between allies and friends broke out when France, Germany and Spain summoned both the UK and US ambassadors to explain the motives behind their surveillance activities. One of the most shocking discoveries from the US spy disclosures was about Britain's Government Communication Headquarters' (GCHQ's) worldwide spying campaign. This top secret surveillance program is called TEMPORA. Now GCHQ wants to extend this surveillance campaign to over 100 states. Another misadventure is a newly expected bill that proposes amendment of the Interception Communication Law and Regu-

---

[1] On 19 June 2012, *Daily Mail* reported that an eminent British doctor told a meeting of the Royal Society of Medicine in London that every year 130,000 elderly patients that die while under the care of the National Health Service (NHS) have been effectively euthanized by being put on the controversial Liverpool Care Pathway (LCP), a protocol for care of the terminally ill that he described as a "death pathway." Dr. Patrick Pullicino, a consultant neurologist for East Kent Hospitals and Professor of Clinical Neurosciences at the University of Kent, claimed that doctors are putting people on the LCP without proper analysis of their condition, citing "pressure on beds and difficulty with nursing confused or difficult-to-manage elderly patients" as factors.

lation of Investigatory Powers Act 2000 (RIPA), 2000 to allow the government to issue interception warrants to telecommunication companies and internet services across the world.[1]

Now citizens understand that their own privacy is being sacrificed in the name of concerns over international security. Cyberspace has also become a decisive arena of modern information warfare. Every morning we find ourselves in a far more dangerous world. With the global spread of technology and international links, we see a rapid rise in the traffic of dangerous ideas, dangerous materials and dangerous people. Short-term fixes are not enough. Real leadership and real solutions are urgently needed. This is a damning aspect of the issue but deep public loathing towards the US spy revelations suggests that, from now, the British government will be unable to protect the privacy and civil liberties of its citizens.

The ongoing violence in Northern Ireland where the political parties failed to agree on a power sharing formula after the Good Friday Agreement, and illicit trade in drugs and nuclear materials in Central and South Asia have further jeopardized the national security of the state. The September 2014 referendum in Scotland has also become a challenging problem. The government's attempts to plug these holes and keep the ship of state moving are entirely inadequate to the scale and scope of challenges as we enter turbulent waters. At the same time, in response to the uprisings that have swept the Arab world, North Africa, Syria and Ukraine, concerns about possible cyber attacks (state-sponsored or otherwise) on state computers or cyber exports have been amplified in the media, sparking a debate as to the appropriate course of action. The performance of several state institutions raised many questions as countless scandals smeared their reputation. The banks lost the trust of both the public and government as a result of their incompetence. Now, British citizens ask, where does the country place itself at this stage of deep crisis and instability?

We are living in a country where corruption and extremism have terminally damaged the smooth functioning of the state.

---

[1] *The Crisis of Surveillance State*, Musa Khan Jalalzai, 2014.

The UK's local governments are under severe criticism due to a growing criminal and bureaucratic culture in borough (district) councils. The weakness and the growing unpopularity of local government, coupled with a decline in confidence and trust on the part of the communities, have received considerable attention from the print and electronic media. Councils have become deeply divided along social, political and sectarian lines. The growing culture of sectarian hate, extremism, jihadism, gunfights, burglaries, low-living standards, decline of the justice system, the brazen attitude of council's officers and their involvement in huge corruption cases are the most challenging problems. Councils are unable to provide housing to poor and vulnerable families and allot houses on political and ethnic bases and, therefore, the hidden homeless have reached about one million.[1]

With the arrival of over one million European immigrants, poverty is in an uncontrollable state. Leaders of all faiths have suggested that local governments take action and tackle the culture of corruption, rising hunger and food shortages. The local government ombudsman has become a controversial figure. The ombudsman uses his discretionary power not to investigate a complaint as a way of covering up maladministration and injustice. When one makes a complaint to any local body of the council, he is faced with a lot of paper work and a plethora of unintelligible language. Trust in local governments is at an all time low where political influence, power and self-gratification are the drivers behind corruption. A local NGO called Shelter has recently exposed the real picture of the London boroughs: "Over 1.7 million households are currently waiting for social housing. Some homeless households — many with dependent children — wait for years in temporary accommodations."[2]

---

[1] Ibid.
[2] *Daily Mail*, 26 March 2016.

CHAPTER 11. THE THREAT OF NUCLEAR, CHEMICAL AND BIOLOGICAL TERRORISM IN EUROPE AND THE UNITED KINGDOM

In April 2016, the main focus of Nuclear Security Summit was on the possibilities of chemical and biological terrorism in Europe, where experts of these weapons are available in large number. There is speculation that Muslim extremist organizations and the Islamic State may possibly carry out nuclear, biological and chemical attacks in European cities. The European parliament warned that sectarian extremist groups based in Europe and Britain have money, and scientists, and can buy dangerous materials to constitute a dirty bomb. The European Parliament (December 2015) warned that:

> ISIL/Daesh has vowed that future strikes will be more lethal and even more shocking. This has prompted experts to warn that the group may be planning to try to use internationally banned weapons of mass destruction in future attacks. On 19 November 2015, the French Prime Minister, Manuel Valls, raised the specter of ISIL/Daesh planning a chemical or biological attack. At present, European citizens are not seriously contemplating the possibility that extremist groups might use chemical, biological, radiological or nuclear (CBRN)

materials during attacks in Europe. Under these circumstances, the impact of such an attack, should it occur, would be even more destabilizing. Several experts have warned that there is a genuine risk of ISIL/Daesh using chemical, biological, radiological or even nuclear materials in the context of future attacks on European targets.[1]

Participants in a nuclear security summit in Washington also warned that the possible use of biological, chemical, radiological and nuclear materials by terrorist organizations like the Islamic State and EU based extremist groups can inflict huge destruction and the loss of human lives. The US President warned that terrorist can target any nuclear and military installation across Europe. On 19 November 2015, the French Prime Minister, Manuel Valls, raised the specter of ISIS planning a chemical or biological attack. There are speculations that terrorist groups may possibly establish their networks within the state institution of some EU member states, and can make access to nuclear and biological weapons.

In Europe, there is the general perception that as extremist and sectarian groups have already used some dangerous gases in Iraq, Afghanistan and Syria; therefore, they could use biological weapons against civilian populations in Britain and Europe. If control over these weapons is weak, or if their components are available in the open market, terrorists can inflict huge fatalities in the region. Holger Muench, President of Germany's Federal Police (BKA), has said that only about half of the European Union's 28 states currently compare fingerprints. "Due to the growth and often fragmented IT architecture, it is currently not possible to systematically bring together the available evidence," lamented Federal Interior Minister Thomas de Maiziere. Deutsche Welle (DW) is Germany's international broadcaster, a reputable news source, has also warned that: "According to the International Centre for the Study of Radicalization at King's College in London, an estimated 500 Belgian nationals have

---

[1] *Chemical Terrorism*, http://ready.navy.mil/content/dam/ReadyNavy/pdfs/beinformedpdfs/terrorism/TERRORISM_Chemical_031015JJK.pdf.

travelled to Syria or Iraq to become fighters for the so-called 'Islamic State'—the highest number per capita in Europe."[1]

Experts recently warned that the availability of such materials in the open markets of some European states can fall in the hand of local terrorist organizations, which may further jeopardize the security of the region. Two Belgian nuclear power plant workers had joined ISIS also leading to fears the jihadists had the intelligence to cause a meltdown disaster. Before the suicide attacks in Belgian, security services were fearful that ISIS operatives may had been looking to target a nuclear plant as it emerged two workers from a plant in Doel fled to Syria to join ISIS. Belgian Interior Minister Jan Jambon said at the time that authorities had determined there was a threat "to the person in question, but not the nuclear facilities.[2]

At the end of summit, the joint statement said: "We believe that since Pakistan has strong credentials on nuclear safety, security and non-proliferation, it qualifies for full integration in the multilateral export control regimes," on one hand, while on the other hand, the Obama administration issued a stern warning to India and Pakistan to insure the security of the nuclear weapons. This inconsistent and contradictory approach of the US government towards Pakistan causes misunderstandings between the two states. Conversely, the statement submitted by Pakistan confirmed that: "Within the framework of these instruments and the IAEA activities and programmes, Pakistan is committed to international cooperation consistent with our national priorities."[3]

---

[1] The United Kingdom Strategy for Countering Chemical, Biological, Radiological and Nuclear Terrorism (CBRN-2010), "radiological material can be combined with explosives to produce a radiological dispersion device (RDD), sometimes called a dirty bomb.

[2] On June 6, 2015, *Pajhwok News* reported that dozens of schoolgirls were targeted by unknown terrorists using biological agents in Panj Aab district of Bamyan province. This could also happen in Punjab, Baluchistan, Sindh and Khyber Pakhtunkhwa or Delhi and Mumbai unless the export control regime is tightened.

[3] Dr Abdul Qadir Khan categorically said that nuclear smuggling activities did take place from 1992 to 1998 while both Nawaz Sharif and Benazir Bhutto were in power. However, Mr. Chaudhry said his country had significantly cracked down on proliferation in recent years, improving its export controls and providing the United Nations Nuclear Monitors with all the necessary information.

The threat of nuclear terrorism and the use of dirty bombs by the terrorist organizations in Britain and Europe cannot be ruled out as these groups have established close relationships with some disgruntled elements within government circles. They have established strong contacts with foreign embassies and terrorist organizations across the borders. The threat is very real, but some irresponsible states do not realize the sensitivity of the situation. The changing nature of the threat and the dramatic rise of the ISIS is matter of great concern for major nuclear powers in Europe. On 19 April, German media reported that ISIS was sending jihadists, dressed as ice-cream salesmen, to beaches where they plan to detonate suicide vests and use high-powered assault rifles to kill indiscriminately. According to BILD the BND, the German MI6, has learned from its Italian intelligence that resorts in southern France, the Costa del Sol in Spain and both coasts in Italy are most under threat.

As the world has entered the era of mass murder techniques, the ISIS and Takfiri terrorist organizations in Britain and Europe are trying to retrieve materials of dirty bomb and inflict maximum possible carnage to achieve their goal. Making a crude bomb for them is not a difficult task as highly professional and technical people joined their ranks, and continue to apply various means in preparing chemical and biological weapons. In many occasions international press reported the insecurity of nuclear materials in Europe, but international community never asked for the improvement of the security of their nuclear installations.

On 20 April 2016, RT reported NATO and EU security chiefs saying Islamic State (IS, formerly ISIS/ISIL) wanted to use chemical or nuclear weapons to attack Britain. During the recent Security and Counter Terror conference in London, a group of policing and counter terrorism experts delivered a dire warning. Jorge Berto Silva, the European Commission's deputy chief of counter-terrorism, told the Telegraph that "with CBRN [chemical, biological, radioactive and nuclear materials], there is a justified concern."RT reported.[1]

---

[1] On June 5, 2015 *Dawn* reported Foreign Secretary Aizaz Ahmad Chaudhry ruled out sharing nuclear secrets with Saudi Arabia, insisting that nuclear assets would continue to serve Pakistan alone. On 20

The National Police Chiefs Council (NPCC) said the number of workers trained to respond to terrorist incidents increased from its current rate of 100,000 employees per year. Detective Chief Superintendent Scott Wilson, police counter-terrorism coordinator, is expected to announce the expansion of Project Griffin in the near future. He told the BBC "we need everyone to play a part in keeping the public alert, not alarmed."[1]

Despite some progress over the past decades, the security of nuclear weapons is in danger as some materials remain dangerously vulnerable to theft. India and Pakistan also continue to expand their nuclear arsenals, now numbering many hundreds of weapons, and are continuing to rely on doctrines likely to lead to early dispersal of those weapons in the event of a crisis. North Korea has 100 nuclear weapons, while Iran continues to develop more dangerous strategies, and is a bigger threat to Afghanistan and the security of the Gulf States.

Cases of nuclear smuggling in some European states indicate that the possibilities of the use of nuclear, chemical and biological weapons cannot be ruled out. The EU is in danger because all member states pose violent threat of nuclear terrorism from the home-grown extremist and terrorist organizations. With so many nuclear explosives held by law enforcement agencies in Europe, international community has long standing worries about the possibilities of nuclear and biological terrorism in the region. The 13th November 2015 terrorist attacks in France and the March 2016 attacks in Brussels, in which terrorists sought to retrieve nuclear weapons raised serious question about the nuclear security of EU member states.[2]

In several EU member states, experts of Improvised Explosive and Nuclear Explosive Devices have come from Pakistan, Afghanistan, Africa and the Arab world who can easily prepare dirty bomb. Chemical weapons have been described as 'the poor

---

April 2016, *RT* reported NATO and EU security chiefs saying Islamic State (IS, formerly ISIS/ISIL) wanted to use chemical or nuclear weapons to attack Britain.

[1] *RT* 20 April 2016.

[2] The 13th November 2015 terrorist attacks in France and the March 2016 attacks in Brussels, in which terrorists sought to retrieve nuclear weapons raised serious question about the nuclear security of EU member states, *The Guardian*, 13 Nov 2013.

man's atomic bomb', an expression which also captures some of the moral and legal taboo which has historically (albeit not universally) been associated with chemical weapons. Although the large-scale production, weaponization and delivery of chemical weapons would be challenging, scientifically and logistically, as well as extremely expensive, a small number of low-yield chemical weapons would be relatively easy to hide and transport and might thus appeal to a well-organized and well-funded terrorist group.[1]

A grave concern for many is the prospect of so-called Islamic State and other terrorist groups obtaining nuclear or radioactive material to produce a nuclear or "dirty bomb" or attacking or sabotaging a nuclear power plant. Terrorists could attack or sabotage nuclear facilities, such as commercial nuclear power plants or research reactors, to cause a release of radioactivity and terrorists could acquire and release radioactive materials in Europe. The distinctive feature of international security in the early twenty-first century, however, is that terrorists can achieve the effect they desire using WMD-related technologies and materials which would barely qualify as a 'weapon' according to the Cold War criteria. Terror is a weapon of weak actors and it has been found to work more often in the cases where state interests are not high, terrorists moderate their use of violence and do not threaten the fundamental values of the coerced society.

Democracies are considered to be more susceptible to coercion and modifying their policies under such circumstances. A highly committed terrorist group could, conceivably, regard the risks associated with amateurish and unsafe 'weaponization' to be worth taking, and might regard 'handling' and 'deployment' as nothing more complicated than carrying a small bag into a crowded sports stadium. However, on 01 April 2016, Telegraph reported British Prime Minister warned that the ISIS was planning to use drones to spray nuclear materials over Western cities. A British official told newspapers that world leaders have already seen the Islamic State is trying to retrieve nuclear, chemical and biological weapons and use it against civilians and nuclear installation in Europe.[2]

---

[1] *The Chatham House Report*, 07 January 2007.
[2] However, on 01 April 2016, *Telegraph* reported British Prime Minister

On 18 September 2015, Rose Gottemoeller, the US under Secretary for Arms Control and International Security in a nuclear security conference warned that nuclear materials are falling in the hands of terrorists:

> The State Department's Counter Nuclear Smuggling Program (CNSP) is struggling to convince international partners to strengthen capacity to investigate nuclear smuggling networks, secure materials in illegal circulation, and prosecute the criminals who are involved. Countries such as Georgia and Moldova are to be commended for their recent arrests of criminals attempting to traffic HEU; significant progress has been made in this area. Unfortunately, continued seizures of weapon-usable nuclear materials indicate that these materials are still available on the black market. In fact, in many countries, it is not illegal to possess or traffic dangerous radioactive or nuclear materials. In some countries where it is illegal, their existing criminal code does not allow for the adequate prosecution or sentencing of the criminals convicted of doing so."[1]

Pakistan is seeking civilian nuclear technology to meet its electricity needs. For this reason, the country entered its seventh round of strategic dialogue with the US, which ended without any result. The US turned down Pakistan's demand of access to civilian nuclear technology and argued for focus on its non-proliferation credentials because the country always suffers from a negative image due to its tenuous nuclear non-proliferation regime. The possibility of a nuclear technology transfer to Saudi Arabia is still reverberating in the press, although on 05 June, 2015, Foreign Secretary Aizaz Ahmad Chaudhry ruled out sharing nuclear secrets with Saudi Arabia, insisting that nuclear as-

---

warned that the ISIS was planning to use drones to spray nuclear materials over Western cities. A British official told newspapers that world leaders have already seen the Islamic State is trying to retrieve nuclear, chemical and biological weapons and use it against civilians and nuclear installation in Europe.

[1] On 18 September 2015, Rose Gottemoeller, the US under Secretary for Arms Control and International Security, in a nuclear security conference warned that nuclear materials are falling in the hands of terrorists, The US Department of State, http://www.state.gov/t/

sets would continue to serve Pakistan alone. The foreign secretary strongly rejected the rumors that Pakistan is about to sell nuclear arms to Saudi Arabia.

In an interview with a local television channel, Dr. Abdul Qadir Khan categorically said that nuclear smuggling activities did take place from 1992 to 1998 while both Mr. Nawaz Sharif and Benazir Bhutto were in power. It means they and the army generals were deeply involved. However, Mr. Chaudhry said his country had significantly cracked down on proliferation in recent years, improving its export controls and providing the United Nations Nuclear Monitors with all the necessary information. Pakistani politicians are confident that the country's army is capable of preventing nuclear weapons from falling into the hands of the Taliban and ISIS. The fear that India and Pakistan could use nuclear weapons against each other in case of a major terror attack has not ebbed. Pakistan says it will not use nuclear weapons against its neighbors without any reason but if India were to do so, the country has the right to respond to an Indian attack.[1]

According to the nuclear doctrine of Pakistan, nuclear weapons would only be used according to the principles therein. At home, Europeans should exchange ideas about the best ways to prevent the radicalization and recruitment of terrorists in their own countries, as well as abroad and online. And governments need to prepare for the unthinkable: the aftermath of a terrorist attack using chemical, biological or radiation-based weapons. Cross border co-operation – such as access to another country's laboratories and medical expertise – could be of critical significance in the wake of such attacks. Any future attack is unlikely to employ a developed chemical weapon such as VX or Sarin gas. The EU's single market is already subject to rules on the security of CBRN materials. For example, there are EU-wide bio-safety standards governing the handling, transport, usage and disposal of biological agents and precursors. Senior research fellow at the

---

[1] *South Asian Monitor*, 09 June 2015, in an interview with a local television channel, Dr. Abdul Qadir Khan categorically said that nuclear smuggling activities did take place from 1992 to 1998 while both Nawaz Sharif and Benazir Bhutto were in power. It means they and the army generals were deeply involved.

Centre for European Reform Hugo Brady in his research paper (Intelligence, emergencies and foreign policy: The EU's role in counter-terrorism) has analyzed the weakness and incompetency of EU policing and intelligence agencies:

> Many intelligence services work on the assumption that Europol is not yet a sufficiently serious outfit to do business with, particularly in ongoing investigations. Europol twice attempted – once before and once after the Madrid bombings – to establish a special office of national counter-terror experts. Both attempts failed. In addition, it has become commonplace to observe that Europol and Eurojust have a tendency to duplicate each others' efforts and still fail to work properly together, despite habitual pressure to do so from their political masters. One reason for such failings is that these two bodies operate in a horrendously complex legal environment. Europol in particular must adhere to an inflexible and dogmatic data protection regime. This means that the office is often held to higher standards than national police forces when sharing information within the EU and with outsiders.[1]

Weapons of Mass Destruction are nuclear, biological and chemical weapons. But are they an alternative to traditional weapons for terrorist attacks? It is undoubtedly true that the use of one single device of such weapons might kill thousands of people in a rather short time. Protection against these weapons is very complicated or even impossible. The use of biological weapons has been alleged on several occasions but not proved. The choice of the bio-warfare agent depends on the economic, technical, and financial capabilities of the state or organization. Smallpox, Ebola, and Marburg virus might be chosen because they have a reputation for causing a more horrifying illness. Images on the nightly news of doctors, nurses, and law enforce-

---

[1] Senior research fellow at the Centre for European Reform Hugo Brady in his research paper (Intelligence, emergencies and foreign policy: The EU's role in counter-terrorism) has analyzed the weakness and incompetency of EU policing and intelligence agencies, Intelligence, emergencies and foreign policy: The EU's role in counter-terrorism, Hugo Brady, The Centre for European Reform

ment personnel in full protective gear could cause widespread public distraction and anxiety. Bio-warfare attacks are now a possibility.

A document from Pakistan's Internal Security Policy (2014–2018) categorically stated that the country's security faces the threat of nuclear terrorism. The threat, according to the document's contents, is in addition to the possibility of chemical and biological terrorism. As the fatal war against terrorism has entered a crucial phase, another powerful extremist militant group (ISIS) has emerged with a strong and well-trained army in Afghanistan and parts of Pakistan to establish an Islamic state. The massacre of 100 innocent civilians, including an Afghan national army soldier in the Ajristan district of Ghazni province, Afghanistan by IS forces, and the brutal killings of children in the army school in Peshawar have raised serious questions about the future of security and stability in South Asia. The Tehreek-e-Taliban Pakistan (TTP) claimed responsibility and called it a revenge attack for the Pakistan army's Operation Zarb-e-Azb in North Waziristan and FATA region.

The terror attacks in Turkey, France, Belgium, Sanai, Beirut and Tunis have already cost the lives of more than 500 people. Threats can emanate from highly qualified individuals who have access to sensitive information and materials, and who possess the necessary expertise. The ISIS controls large swathes of territory, approximately the size of Belgium, stretching, in Syria, from near the Turkish border to close to the Lebanese border, and to the east, in Iraq, to close to Baghdad.

The problem of nuclear and biological terrorism deserves special attention from the governments of Pakistan and Afghanistan because the army of ISIS can develop a dirty bomb in which explosives can be combined with a radioactive source like those commonly used in hospitals or extractive industries. The use of this weapon might have severe health effects, causing more disruption than destruction. Political and military circles in Pakistan fear that, as IS has already seized chemical weapons in Al Muthanna, in northern Iraq, some disgruntled retired military officers or experts in nuclear explosive devices might help the Pakistan chapter of the group deploy biological and chemical weapons. A letter by the Iraqi government to the UN warned that the militant-captured chemical weapons site contains 2,500 chemical rockets filled with the nerve agent Sarin.

Most of the declared chemical weapons (CW) material has been removed from Syria in the past few months and destroyed. However, there are indications that some material still remains in the country and is potentially accessible to ISIL. In addition, the Organization for the Prohibition of Chemical Weapons (OPCW) suggested that chemical material not qualifying as CW and not subject to being declared under the CW convention, such as chlorine, has actually been used by the Assad regime in the fight against the Syrian opposition. Some press reports indicate that ISIL might have done the same.

The Islamic State have access to nuclear and biological weapons and nerve gas that remained in Syria, as well as mustard agents and nerve agent rockets from Iraq, and obtained chemical weapon components from Iraq and banned and undeclared chemical weapon stockpiles from Syria. It is primarily the responsibility of Member States to protect the population against CBRN incidents. The EU has no law to specifically target or seek to control chemical, biological, radiological and nuclear substances that could be used as ingredients of weapons of mass destruction. The European Union legislation is restricted to controlling the use of chemicals as explosives precursors. Regulation (EU) No 98/2013 on the marketing and use of explosives precursors.

In Europe, there is the general perception that IS has already used some dangerous gases in Iraq. Therefore, it could use biological weapons against civilian populations in Pakistan. If control over these weapons is weak, or if their components are available in the open market, there would be huge destruction in the region. In July 2014, the government of Iraq notified that nuclear material had been seized by the IS army from Mosul University. IS has a 19-page document in Arabic on how to develop biological weapons, and a 26-page religious fatwa that allows the use of weapons of mass destruction. "If Muslims cannot defeat the kafir (non-believers) in a different way, it is permissible to use weapons of mass destruction," warns the fatwa.[1]

---

[1] In July 2014, the government of Iraq notified that nuclear material had been seized by the IS army from Mosul University. IS has a 19-page doc-

The effects of chemical weapons are worse as they cause death or incapacitation, while biological weapons cause death or disease in humans, animals or plants. We have two international treaties that ban the use of such weapons. Notwithstanding all these preventive measures, the threat of chemical or biological warfare persists. In 2011 and 2013, there were complaints and allegations that some states wanted to target Pakistan with biological weapons. The country has been trying to counter biological attacks but has failed due to limited funds and medical knowledge. As Pakistan noted in its statement to the Meeting of States Parties in December 2013: "Pakistan ratified the Biological and Toxic Weapons Convention (BTWC) in 1974 as a non-possessor state and remains fully committed to implementing all provisions of the convention."[1]

The Islamic State (ISIS) is armed with biological and chemical weapons but Europeans don't take the existential threat seriously, according to a European Union parliament document. ISIS has been trafficking in chemical weapons and also is able to manufacture them by putting together a team of experts with degrees in chemistry and physics. Terror can worsen in Europe, whether it is because of terrorists who are there now or because of those who be recruited in the future. In August 2015, 35 Kurdish fighters were wounded in a chemical attack whilst fighting ISIS terrorists near Erbil, a source from the OPCW (Organization for the Prohibition of Chemical Weapons) said that laboratory tests revealed that mustard gas had been used.[2]

As long as the threat of nuclear terrorism exists, the effort to secure and reduce weapons usable nuclear and radiological materials must continue. Efforts to continue improving nuclear security measures include holding regular expert and industry meetings as well as meetings between senior government officials. The challenge for terrorist groups then becomes getting hold of a sufficient amount of nuclear material for an effective bomb, while countries with nuclear facilities need to "protect the material at the source. This is not currently being done to

---

ument in Arabic on how to develop biological weapons, and a 26-page religious fatwa that allows the use of weapons of mass destruction.
[1] *The Prospect of Nuclear Jihad in Pakistan*, Musa Khan Jalalzai, 2015.
[2] Ibid.

a high enough standard, according to the expert, who claims atomic material can currently "be easily found. There is a black market where such material is available coming from central and Eastern Europe. The consequences of even a single act of nuclear terrorism would be catastrophic. Serious and sustained work to combat this threat is in our common interest and must continue to be a global collective priority.

The risk of the use of nuclear weapons or of nuclear or radio-active material by terrorists only began to be acknowledged as a real threat at the beginning of the 21st century. The Convention for the Physical Protection of Nuclear Material was therefore expended under Austrian leadership. The United Nations Security Council adopted Resolution 1540 (2004), binding all States to prevent the proliferation of (nuclear, chemical and biological) weapons of mass destruction, as well as their means of delivery to non-state actors. The resolution is implemented both at national as well as at EU-level. An international summit on nuclear security in Washington discussed the agenda to stop terrorist organizations such as the Islamic State group from getting their hands on nuclear material. But how real is the threat? In the aftermath of the November 13 2015 terror attacks in Paris, and with the eyes of the world still focused on the bloodshed in the French capital, soldiers in Belgium were sent to guard the country's nuclear power plants.[1]

Four months after the terrorist attacks, Belgium found itself in the crosshairs as terrorists killed 32 people in the March 22 suicide bombings in Brussels. Moments after the attacks, the country's two large-scale nuclear power plants at Tihange and Doel were completely closed off and virtually all employees sent home. "The terrorists intended to take the physicist's family hostage to force him to steal radioactive material from his laboratory," claimed France's L'Express newspaper, citing

---

[1] The United Nations Security Council adopted Resolution 1540 (2004), binding all States to prevent the proliferation of (nuclear, chemical and biological) weapons of mass destruction, as well as their means of delivery to non-state actors. The resolution is implemented both at national as well as at EU-level. An international summit on nuclear security in Washington discussed the agenda to stop terrorist organizations such as the Islamic State group from getting their hands on nuclear material. *The UN, Committee No 1540*

police sources. Their intention would have been to make a so-called "dirty bomb," where radioactive material is added to conventional explosives to radioactively contaminate an area. The challenge for terrorist groups then becomes getting hold of a sufficient amount of nuclear material for an effective bomb, while countries with nuclear facilities need to "protect the material at the source.[1]

The threat of chemical, biological and nuclear terrorism in South Asia also causes deep frustration and anxiety, as the region hosts many militant organizations. These groups have already learnt the technique of making nuclear explosive devices and the illegal transactions of poorly protected materials remain a threat. The Subcontinent is the most volatile region because India and Pakistan are engaged in a dangerous nuclear arms race. India is enjoying conventional superiority. The addition of a nuclear dimension to this conflict is a matter of great concern. India's National Security Advisor admitted in one of his recent speeches that a fourth generation war is being fought against Pakistan with different tactics and dimensions. Strategically speaking, India and Pakistan have their own threat perceptions, which are quite similar. India wants to be a strong nuclear state because of its fear of Chinese aggression, while Pakistan also needs nuclear weapons because of its fear of Indian aggression. China helps Pakistan in upgrading its nuclear weapons and provides sophisticated weapons to the country's army, while the US helps India.

The misinterpretation of each other's motives has also caused misunderstandings. First they threaten each other with nuclear bombs and then assess the consequences and fatalities. This issue has also been highlighted in a recently published book by Nathan E Busch: "Due to continual mistrust between the two countries, each would be likely to misinterpret military movements, missiles tests, or accidental detonations as an impending attack by the other side. The risks of misinterpreting each other's

---

[1] "The terrorists intended to take the physicist's family hostage to force him to steal radioactive material from his laboratory," claimed a report in France's *L'Express* newspaper, citing police sources. Their intention would have been to make a so-called "dirty bomb", where radioactive material is added to conventional explosives to radioactively contaminate an area, the newspaper speculated. France24 01 April 2016.

motives are compounded by the vulnerabilities of their nuclear forces and the short flight times of the forces to key targets."[1]

The jihadist organizations in South Asia, and even the Islamic State (ISIS) and Taliban, have already demonstrated their interest in retrieving chemical and nuclear weapons, but at present, there is no evidence of their attempts to get access to these weapons. IS recently claimed that it is engaged with Pakistan for nuclear weapons delivery, but this cannot be confirmed through any research papers or news reports. There are confirmed reports that IS retrieved chemical weapons from Iraq and jihadist groups in South Asia are struggling to obtain chemical weapons capability.

For the past six years, improving nuclear security has been part of a high level international undertaking led by President Obama. In 2009, Mr. Obama deemed nuclear terrorism "the most immediate and extreme threat to global security" and called for "a new international effort to secure all vulnerable nuclear material around the world within four years." This work has culminated in a fourth and final Nuclear Security Summit held today in Washington DC, where over 50 heads of states will meet to discuss progress. Since the 2010 inaugural nuclear security summit, steps have been taken to secure and remove weapons-grade materials from potentially vulnerable locations. These include strengthening national border controls to reduce illicit trafficking; removing all weapons useable nuclear material (Highly Enriched Uranium or plutonium) in 14 countries; removing or disposing of 3.2 tons of other nuclear materials; and upgrading the

---

[1] Strategically speaking, India and Pakistan have their own threat perceptions, which are quite similar. India wants to be a strong nuclear state because of its fear of Chinese aggression, while Pakistan also needs nuclear weapons because of its fear of Indian aggression. China helps Pakistan in upgrading its nuclear weapons and provides sophisticated weapons to the country's army, while the US helps India. The misinterpretation of each other's motives has also caused misunderstandings. First they threaten each other with nuclear bombs and then assess the consequences and fatalities. This issue has also been highlighted in a recently published book by Nathan E Busch: "Due to continual mistrust between the two countries, each would be likely to misinterpret military movements, missiles tests, or accidental detonations as an impending attack by the other side. *No End in Sight: The Continuing Menace of Nuclear Proliferation*, Nathan E. Busch, University Press of Kentucky, 2015.

physical security at 32 buildings which store weapons-usable nuclear materials.

A terrorist attack with an improvised nuclear device would create political, economic, social, psychological, and environmental havoc around the world, no matter where the attack occurs. The threat is global, the impact of a nuclear terrorist attack would be global, and the solutions therefore must be global. World leaders have no greater responsibility than ensuring their people and neighboring countries are safe by securing nuclear materials and preventing nuclear terrorism. Two Belgian nuclear power plant workers had joined ISIS leading to fears the jihadism had the intelligence to cause a meltdown disaster.

Belgian security services were fearful that ISIS operatives may have been looking to target a nuclear plant as it emerged two workers from a plant in Doel fled to Syria to join ISIS. One of the men, reportedly known as Ilyas Boughalab, was killed in Syria, while the second served a short prison sentence in Belgium for terror-related offences in 2014. With an extensive understanding of nuclear facilities, the convict's short jail sentence has raised further questioned of the Belgian security services as well as fears he may have passed on important knowledge about the sites to the terrorist group.[1]

According to the New York Times, several employees working in the Belgian nuclear industry have had their security clearances revoked over potential ISIS plots. Belgian Interior Minister Jan Jambon said at the time that authorities had determined there was a threat "to the person in question, but not the nuclear facilities, "according to The Independent. The presumed goal of the suspected ISIS operatives was to obtain enough radioactive material to build a "dirty bomb."[2]

The threat of a nuclear disaster at the hands of terrorists is a global concern and one that requires all of the major players in the nuclear community to be involved in presenting and implementing solutions cooperatively. The risk to reward ratio for attacking nuclear targets has typically been high due to increased security measures taken over the last 15 years and most recently during the series of Nuclear Security Summits initiated by the

---

[1] *Sky News* 26 March 2016.
[2] *CBS News* 22 March 2016.

Obama administration starting in 2010. However, attacks on infrastructure projects such as a nuclear facility need not induce some type of radiological disaster.

Taking a nuclear facility offline could very likely do significant economic damage as these facilities provide base-load electricity to major population centers, many of which do not have adequate spare capacity. Most experts consider additional screening and follow-up with workers and access at nuclear facilities, not only necessary, but also imperative. There is a large consensus in the nuclear security community that nuclear facilities need to conduct and maintain more thorough background checks.

CHAPTER 12. THE PROSPECT OF CHEMICAL AND BIOLOGICAL JIHAD

Recent debates in the print and electronic media about the possible use of chlorine bombs or biological weapons in the EU and UK have caused deep concerns in government and military circles that the radicalized jihadists returning to the region from Syria may possibly use these weapons. Yet experts have warned that the acquisition of nuclear weapons by the terrorists of Islamic State (ISIS) poses a greater threat to the national security of the UK. A variety of chemical may be dangerous including— nerve agents, mustard gases and choking agents. Others are used in industry, or made from natural or everyday household materials. Some chemical agents are difficult to produce, but the potential for release by terrorist attack existed anywhere hazardous industrial or military chemicals are stored. Chemical agents can produce effects quickly (within a few seconds) or slowly (as much as two days after exposure), and some are odorless and tasteless.[1]

Certain chemical agents can also be delivered covertly through contaminated food or water. In 1999, the vulnerability of the food supply was illustrated in Belgium, when chickens were unintentionally exposed to dioxin-contaminated fat used

---

[1] Ready Navy, http://www.ready.navy.mil/be_informed/terrorism/chemical_terrorism.html.

to make animal feed. Because the contamination was not discovered for months, the dioxin a cancer-causing chemical that does not cause immediate symptoms in humans, was probably present in chicken meat and eggs sold in Europe during early 1999. This incident underscores the need for prompt diagnoses of unusual or suspicious health problems in animals as well as humans, a lesson that was also demonstrated by the recent outbreak of mosquito borne West Nile virus in birds and humans in New York City in 1999. The dioxin episode also demonstrates how a covert act of food borne biological or chemical terrorism could affect commerce and human or animal health.[1]

It is difficult to deliver chemical agents in lethal concentrations, and—outdoors—agents often dissipate rapidly. Most of these chemical agents are in storage facilities. Comparing nuclear facilities, biological research laboratories, and chemical agent storage sites, the chemical agent storage sites would be easiest to penetrate. At some sites, the chemicals have been stored for so long that the security personnel do not even know what is being guarded.

The gravest danger arises from the access of extremist and terror groups to the state-owned nuclear, biological and chemical weapons of Iraq and Syria. The growing use of chlorine bombs became a matter of concern when a former commander of the Joint Chemical, Biological, Radiological and Nuclear Regiment told The Times that the UK needed to take strong security measures and control the availability of chemical weapons such as chlorine bombs to the terrorists. Counterterrorism expert Olivier Guitta told The Times that the threat of improvised chemical bombs was also increasing.

> The chemicals and equipment necessary for such preparation are easily purchased; their purchase should not arouse any suspicions concerning their ultimate use; and...Fluoroacetate compounds with much greater specific toxicity than, for example, commercial compounds based on sodium fluoroacetate, may be prepared for use

[1] *Weapons of Mass Casualties and Terrorism Response Handbook*, American Academy of Orthopedic Surgeons Monograph Series, Charles Edward Stewart, American Academy of Orthopedic Surgeons, Jones & Bartlett Learning, 2006.

in chemical weapons. The first such incident was that of ISIS commanders gaining access to the Iraqi nuclear weapons site in Mosul University. Recent cases of nuclear proliferation and attacks on nuclear installations across the globe have further exacerbated the concern about the threat of nuclear attacks in the UK, Pakistan and Afghanistan. The threat of chemical and biological jihad in the UK has raised serious questions about the security of its nuclear weapons. Experts have warned that the UK-based, IS-trained jihadists, the Taliban and Bengali, Afghani, Somali, Nigerian, Arab and Pakistani extremist groups pose a great security threat.

Improvised explosive devices and chemical and biological weapons are easily available in some Asian and African markets and can be transported to the EU and UK through human traffickers. The influx of trained terrorists and organized criminals from several Asian, African and European states has raised concerns that these people who sought asylum through fake documents, or tried to gain citizenship through marriages, could pose a threat to the country. According to the UK Strategy for Countering Chemical, Biological, Radiological and Nuclear Terrorism (CBRN-2010), "radiological material can be combined with explosives to produce a radiological dispersion device (RDD), sometimes called a dirty bomb which will contaminate people, and buildings."[1]

In his recent dossier, William McNeill warned that the UK Trident system is not very secure. He also reported a host of minor breakdowns and faults, which could be resolved, but there are some issues that require serious investigation. As examples he mentioned some unreported incidents, like the collisions of British and French nuclear weapons submarines. The threat of chemical and biological weapons further intensified when British Home Secretary Theresa May warned that members of IS are trying to acquire nuclear weapons to attack the west. She also

---

[1] According to the United UK Strategy for Countering Chemical, Biological, Radiological and Nuclear Terrorism (CBRN-2010), radiological material can be combined with explosives to produce a radiological dispersion device (RDD), sometimes called a dirty bomb, which will contaminate people, and buildings.

warned that jihadists in the UK want to acquire nuclear and biological weapons to be used within the country. Experts in London have warned that these threats should not be considered small or insignificant.

In a press conference in Australia, President Obama declared that if his government discovered that IS had come to possess a nuclear weapon, he would get it out of their hands. The fear of such attacks still exists in the UK and EU because more than 6,000 British and European nationals have joined IS's military campaign in Syria and Iraq. The British law enforcement and intelligence community's fear that the terrorist group can buy nuclear weapons from the black market or any irresponsible state is justified because IS has reportedly developed nuclear weapons using radioactive materials stolen from an Iraqi university.

In 2013, chemical attacks in the outskirts of Damascus posed a direct threat to the US and its allies, causing the UN Security Council to adopt a resolution on chemical weapons in Syria. The international operation of transporting the components of these weapons out of Syria was completed in the first half of 2014. In 2015, IS tried to gain access to these weapons in Syria and, in some cases, used chlorine bombs for terrorist activities in Iraq and Syria. On January 6, 2015, cases of ISIS using chemical weapons in Iraq and Syria emerged. These chemical attacks illustrate that IS and the Syrian opposition chose to use chemical weapons preferentially in Iraq and Syria. In Pakistan and Afghanistan as well, ISIS is seeking these weapons to use them against the armed forces. In the latest issue of its magazine (Dabiq), Islamic State claimed that it wants to buy nuclear weapons from Pakistan but experts view this claim as baseless, saying that a country likes Pakistan would never allow IS to purchase nuclear weapons from the country.

Military experts and policymakers have also expressed deep concerns that if ISIS gains nuclear explosives or some states give it to their favorite terror groups, it might cause huge destruction and casualties for the civilian populations and military installations. Recent events in Paris and Belgium have raised the prospect of extremist and jihadist groups using biological, radiological and chemical attacks against military installations and critical national infrastructure in both states. The two states are vulnerable to such attacks by the Islamic State.

The greatest threat to the national security of Pakistan and India stems from nuclear smuggling and terror groups operating in Punjab, Baluchistan, Assam and Kashmir. Increasingly sophisticated chemical and biological weapons are accessible to organizations like IS, Mujahedeen-e-Hind (MH), and the Taliban and their allies, which is a matter of great concern. These groups can use more sophisticated conventional weapons as well as chemical and biological agents in India and Pakistan in the near future, as they have already experimented in Iraq and Syria. They can disperse chemical, biological and radiological material as well as industrial agents via water or land to target schools, colleges, civilian and military personnel. On June 6, 2015, Pajhwok News reported that dozens of schoolgirls were targeted by unknown terrorists using biological agents in Panj Aab district of Bamyan province. This could also happen in Punjab, Baluchistan, Sindh and Khyber Pakhtunkhwa or Delhi and Mumbai unless the export control regime is tightened.[1]

As international media focuses on the looming threat of chemical and biological terrorism in Asia and Europe, ISIS is seeking nuclear weapons but retrieving these weapons from the country is not an easy task. Pakistan has established a strong nuclear force to safeguard all nuclear sites 24 hours a day with modern military technology. The crisis is going to get worse as the exponential network of IS and its popularity in Afghanistan creates deep security challenges for Pakistan and its Taliban allies. This group could use chemical and biological weapons once it gains footing in Afghanistan.

For this reason, Pakistan is trying to push the Afghan Taliban towards a political settlement in Afghanistan to prevent IS from gaining control of the country. IS and the Taliban are not the only security challenges for Pakistan; the country is also facing many social and economic problems, including electricity shortages. The possibility of a nuclear technology transfer to Saudi Arabia is still reverberating in the press, although on June 5,

---

[1] On June 6, 2015, Pajhwok News reported that dozens of schoolgirls were targeted by unknown terrorists using biological agents in Panj Aab district of Bamyan province. This could also happen in Punjab, Baluchistan, Sindh and Khyber Pakhtunkhwa or Delhi and Mumbai unless the export control regime is tightened.

2015, Foreign Secretary Aizaz Ahmad Chaudhry ruled out sharing nuclear secrets with Saudi Arabia, insisting that nuclear assets would continue to serve Pakistan alone. The foreign secretary strongly rejected the rumors that Pakistan is about to sell nuclear arms to Saudi Arabia.[1]

Pakistani politicians are confident that the country's army is capable of preventing nuclear weapons from falling into the hands of the Taliban and IS. The fear that India and Pakistan could use nuclear weapons against each other in case of a major terror attack has not ebbed. Pakistan says it will not use nuclear weapons against its neighbors without any reason but if India were to do so, the country has the right to respond to an Indian attack. According to the nuclear doctrine of Pakistan, nuclear weapons would only be used according to the principles therein. India's policymakers are facing a strategic conundrum about how to undermine or respond to the terrorist threat emanating from Pakistan and Afghanistan. In 2002 and 2008, both Atal Bihari Vajpayee and Manmohan Singh's governments faced an unstable situation in India. The issue of the Cold Start doctrine and the possibility of a sudden Indian nuclear attack in Pakistan have been elucidated in a recently published research paper:

> Today, Indian military analysts also increasingly recognize the risk of even limited ground operation, not withstanding initial excitement over the more finely calibrated plans proffered by proponents of the so called 'Cold Start' doctrine, similar to the ground option, with Indian forces limiting the depth of their thrust so as not to cross Pakistan's nuclear red lines. Yet, even a limited response that puts Indian boots on Pakistani soil could quickly escalate to major operations that would result in more casualties than would have been suffered in the initial terrorist attack. And, the more Indian forces were succeeding on Pakistani territory, the greater the incentive Pakistan leaders would feel to use nuclear weapons to repulse them.[2]

---

[1] June 5, 2015, Foreign Secretary Aizaz Ahmad Chaudhry ruled out sharing nuclear secrets with Saudi Arabia, insisting that nuclear assets would continue to serve Pakistan alone. *Dawn*, Islamabad, Pakistan.

[2] George Perkovich and Toby Dalton, "Modi's Strategic Choice," *The Washington Quarterly*. Spring 2015

However, experts say that India does not have the capability to carry out a special operation inside Pakistan with precision air support. Pakistan has a strong air force and has adorned its submarines with nuclear weapons. In February 2012, the country announced that it had started work on the construction of nuclear submarines to better meet the Indian navy's nuclear threat. The current threat of nuclear, biological and chemical weapons proliferation signals trouble, particularly in the Middle East and South Asia, which will not be redressed without resolving regional conflicts, which may in turn require internal political changes. India and Pakistan need to implement nuclear risk reduction measures. Terrorists want to buy or steal nuclear material to fabricate a crude bomb or to make or detonate radiological weapons.

CHAPTER 13. PAKISTAN AND BIOLOGICAL WEAPONS

by Dr. Dany Shoham

Pakistan is a state party to the Biological Weapons Convention, yet at least part of its related outward conduct is rather exhibitory, aiming to foster the image of an obedient, sheer science- and protection-oriented profile. Although it is publicly accentuated that an ongoing Pakistani biological weapons (BW) program cannot be proved, it is fairly clear that some Western intelligence agencies possess classified information that is highly supportive of such an active program taking place in actuality. The biotechnological and biomedical infrastructures of Pakistan evidently enable such program. An active BW program in all likelihood commenced in Pakistan in the 1980s, and it possibly yielded a first generation BW arsenal by 1994. Otherwise, a first generation BW arsenal probably came into being during the second half of the 1990s or the first half of the 2000s. Ongoing development and upgrading have been observed, underlying a significant Pakistani sub-nuclear weapon of mass destruction capability.

Introduction

Biological weapons are distinguishable for outlining four fundamental dualities. The first is that the borderline ostensibly separating civilian oriented and military-oriented biotechnologies/purposes is often invisible, and rather does not exist. The second one similarly applies, militarily, to defensive and offensive purposes. A third duality pertains to the strategic importance of BW possession for a country with an unfavorable geopolitical and/or military position, which does not possess nuclear weapons (NW), hence, the need to rely on sub-nuclear weapons of mass destruction (WMD); or conversely, it does possess NW, and might feel more confident to maintain and employ BW, already having the nuclear backup. The fourth duality is in that—albeit shaped in the form of weapons—pathogens can be employed in a manner that would outwardly fully emulate a natural outbreak of an infectious disease, leaving the afflicted incapable of proving whether and by whom they were attacked.

Possessing NW capability since the 1980s, Pakistan is plausibly inclined to pursue sub-nuclear WMD too, which is (presently and in the past) the case with most countries armed with NW. In general, such inclination makes sense conceptually as well, as mentioned above, either regarding a state in or not in possession of NW, due to an unfavorable geopolitical and/or military position. Moreover, it is nearly self-evident that a country that succeeded in domestically developing operational NW—whether with or without foreign assistance—would be capable, in terms of technological capacities, to successfully develop operational BW too. All this would apply to Pakistan.

Westwards, the Pakistani perspective and interfaces pertaining to the Muslim block are of relevance as well. For long, already, Pakistan is in that sense an additional sister link, alongside with Egypt (the first one to run BW and chemical weapons [CW] programs since the 1960s), Syria (irrespective of the chemical disarmament now taking place in that country), Iran and Sudan. During the 1980s—when BW and CW programs were apparently launched by Pakistan—Iraq and Libya were in a similar position, namely, endeavoring to construct capabilities of CW, BW and NW altogether. Eastwards, however, the Pakistani interfaces with India and China are no less significant, obviously, within that context at large. Collectively then, the resultant working hypothesis of this article is that Pakistan indeed launched a BW program and has been implementing it. Various

factual and analytical components, as herewith presented, support and corroborate this working hypothesis, although readers
should keep in mind that Pakistan is a party to the 1972 Biological Weapons and Toxin Convention (BWC). The information
covered for that purpose in the present study pertains to strategic, scientific and technological aspects altogether.

Pakistan's Attitude towards the BWC

Pakistan signed the Biological Weapons Convention in
1972—the year it was established—and two years later ratified
it. At that temporal phase, Pakistan was not yet involved practically within the BW sphere. Much later, however, and for a long
period of time, Pakistan has unwillingly been at the forefront
of the BWC negotiations, mainly due to maintaining interfaces
with terror organizations that pursue WMD.[1] As a result, Pakistan's conducts within the various forums of the BWC included
an impressive range of statements and postures which, in themselves, would ostensibly remove any suspicion about concomi-
tantly running a BW program.

This distinctive profile has been taking shape since the
Fourth BWC Review Conference of 1996, shortly after Pakistan
carried out its First National Seminar on Defense against Chemical and Biological Weapons in 1995,[2] and not too long after being pointed at as a country running a productive BW program.[3]
That profile initially relied (in 1996) on a theological motive:

> Islamic laws of war forbid the use of poisonous
> weapons. For Pakistan, the 1925 Geneva Protocol and
> the Biological and Toxin Weapons Convention are a
> manifestation of a moral and cultural ethos that is over
> 1400 years old. Violations of the prohibition against

---

[1] Revill, J. and Dando, M., 'The Evolution of Pakistan's Approach to
Biological Weapons Non-Proliferation Regime', in Zulfqar Khan (ed.),
Nuclear Pakistan: Strategic Dimensions, Pakistan: Oxford University Press,
2012, pp. 157–88.
[2] *Saudi Gazette*, 28 April 1995, as cited in 'Chemical Weapons Convention
Bulletin', No. 28, June 1995, p. 30.
[3] Collins, John M., Davis, Zachary S., and Bowman, Steven R., 'Nuclear,
Biological, and Chemical Weapon Proliferation: Potential Military
Countermeasures', Congressional Research Service Report No. 94-528
S, Washington, DC: US Government Printing Office, 1994.

the production or use of poisonous weapons should be treated with equal determination in all cases, without selectivity or discrimination.[1]

Since the 2001 Fifth BWC Review Conference onwards, different elements were included in the Pakistani statements and postures; it would be worthwhile to mention the following:[2]

1. With reference to Pakistani capabilities and facilities:

We have a growing academic and research infrastructure. We have a large pool of scientists who are doing important work in the application of biotechnology in the fields of heath, agriculture and food processing. Pakistan's National Institute for Biotechnology and Genetic Engineering (NIGEBE); Centre for Advanced Molecular Biology; and the Nuclear Institute for Agriculture and Biology, are pioneer institutions for research in medicine and agriculture. Interestingly, the three above-mentioned Pakistani facilities represent two out of the four biological entities sanctioned in 1998 by the United States (US) (while the other two became non-existent, seemingly, as detailed later), plus a third facility which is affiliated with the Pakistan Atomic Energy Commission (PAEC).

2. With reference to the Chinese proposals regarding the subject of technical and scientific cooperation:

This Conference must consider the subject of technical and scientific cooperation thoroughly, reaffirming the importance of full implementation of Article X. In this regard, the Chinese proposals, contained in document BWC/Ad Hoc Group/ WP.453, dated May 8, 2001, provide a solid basis for evolving suitable recommendations.

3. With reference to the general status of the convention and its implementation:

---

[1] The Biological and Toxin Weapons Convention, available at http://www.opbw.org/
[2] Ibid.

Pakistan is fully committed to the obligations under the BWC. Pakistan has made significant progress in biotechnology. The BWC is a key disarmament treaty that underpins the international security architecture. It should become a framework for cooperation among nations to eliminate biological weaponization and to fight bio-terrorism. The Implementation Support Unit will harness resources, force connections, develop networks and identify opportunities... It will make an important and innovative contribution to our collective effort to reduce the terrible threat posed by biological weapons.

4. With reference to dual use of biological resources:

Rapid developments in the life sciences and life-enhancing breakthroughs in biotechnology have opened new horizons in medicine, health, agriculture, industry and commerce. These advances are creating opportunities to promote applications of scientific discoveries for peaceful purposes under Article X. We should agree on measures for enhanced international cooperation in peaceful biotechnological activities. This would facilitate economic and social development and strengthen implementation of the Convention.

Developments in the life sciences also have the potential of creating new tools of warfare. The BWC regime needs to control the potentially destructive use of such technologies. Security and oversight of pathogens and mechanisms for disease surveillance and response are urgently required. We need to maintain a balance between negative applications of biosciences and development of technology for peaceful and legitimate purposes. The scientific community is a key player in reducing the risks of the dual-use potential of various technologies. Codes of conduct should aim at preserving the benign uses and stemming the malign uses of biosciences.

5. With reference to the balance between biosafety plus biosecurity and scientific development in biotechnology and genetic engineering:

Pakistan strongly believes that concrete and effective measures should be taken to strengthen biosafety and biosecurity, but at the same time these measures should not hamper the scientific development in biotechnology and genetic engineering. Dealing with the safety and security of biological resources, as well as ensuring that all those involved in relevant activities are aware of the international, regional and national measures which regulate their activities and the principles that underpin them, will go a long way towards ensuring that we continue to enjoy the benefits of biotechnology while being shielded from its dangers. The position of Pakistan in regard to the topics being considered is as follows:

1. Biosafety and biosecurity are not limited to the physical security of laboratories, pathogens and toxins. They encompass risk awareness, measures to ensure that life sciences are committed to their benign use, and protection of knowhow and technology against bioterrorism and biological warfare.

2. A reliable biosafety–biosecurity system would have adequate elements of preparedness and response in the event of deliberate or accidental releases, and an effective disease surveillance mechanism at the national, regional and international levels. Two notable documents submitted by Pakistan to the BWC forums, in addition, are:

1. Perspective on Oversight, Codes of Conduct, Education and Awareness Raising [Document WP.5].[1]

2. The report on "Results of activities to promote universalization of the BWC undertaken by the

---

[1] BWC/MSP/2008/MX/WP.5 document at https://documents-dds-ny.un.org/doc/UNDOC/GEN/G08/625/38/PDF/G0862538.pdf?OpenElement

Chairman and the Implementation Support Unit (ISU) (report).

Results of activities to promote universalization of the BWC undertaken by the Chairman and the Implementation Support Unit (ISU) (report). In a statement to the BWC Review Conference of 2011, Pakistan announced that it had drafted a single law that would 'comprehensively prohibit designing, development, manufacturing, stockpiling, transport, import, export, sale, acquisition and possession of biological agents and toxins including their means of delivery.'[1] Overall, during the various BWC review conferences, Pakistani representatives have urged more robust participation from state signatories, invited new states to join the treaty and, as part of the Non-Aligned Movement, argued in favor of guaranteeing states' rights to engage in peaceful exchanges of biological and toxin materials for scientific research. Unsurprisingly, at least part of the Pakistani conduct is rather exhibitory, aiming to foster the image of sheer science and a protection-oriented profile. Connectedly, it has been observed:

> Whilst such steps are encouraging and commendable, it is not clear the extent to which proclamations have manifest in practice, and Pakistan's unique geostrategic context necessitates that such measures need to be effectively implemented, enforced, and adequately resourced in terms of both political will and economic resources.[2]

Domestic Approaches and Conducts: Mechanisms, Preparedness and Outlooks

The National Command Authority (NCA) of Pakistan is the apex civilian-led command that oversees the policy formulation, exercises, deployment, employment, research and development, and operational command and control of the state's strategic

---

[1] Statement by Ambassador Zamir Akram, Permanent Representative of Pakistan to the United Nations, at the Seventh BWC Review Conference, Permanent Mission of Pakistan to the United Nations, 6 December 2011, available at www.opbw.org.
[2] Revill and Dando, 'The Evolution of Pakistan's Approach to Biological Weapons Non-Proliferation Regime', n. 1, p. 181

forces, including nuclear and presumably sub-nuclear WMD, plus defense against those weapons. The NCA is responsible for control over all related strategic organizations and systems. The Prime Minister (PM) is a Chairman of the NCA, with all components of NCA, military assets and strategic commands directly reporting to the Chairman of their course of development and deployment.

The NCA consists of an Employment Control Committee and a Development Control Committee, as well as the Strategic Plans Division (SPD), which acts as its Secretariat. Among the NCA members are the Director-General of Strategic Planning Directorate (within the SPD), the Minister of Science and Technology and the Chairman of Joint Chiefs of Staff Committee. The latter committee is the highest military body for considering all problems bearing on the military aspects of national defense and rendering professional military advice thereon; it is mainly responsible for preparing joint strategic plans and providing strategic direction. In addition, the PAEC is part of the NCA. The PAEC is the largest science and technology organization of the country, both in terms of scientific/technical manpower and in terms of the scope of its activities.[1]

Within the PAEC, there is a Biosciences Division (also named as the Agriculture and Biotechnology Division), which controls several institutes dealing, among other things, with various pathogens. It can be assumed that this division influences Pakistan's concept regarding BW. Thus the administrative core components involved in shaping the concept and capabilities of Pakistan in the field of biological warfare would appear to include:

1. The Strategic Plans Division (within the NCA)
2. The Development Control Committee (within the NCA)
3. Pakistan Atomic Energy Commission (PAEC)
4. The Bioscience Division (within PAEC)
5. Defense Science and Technology Organization
6. The Directorate of Scientific and Technical Cooperation
7. Ministry of Defense
8. The Joint Chiefs of Staff Committee

---

[1] See http://en.wikipedia.org/wiki/National_Command_Authority_ (Pakistan)

9. Army Medical Corps
10. Ministry of Science and Technology

In practice, it was in April 1995 that Pakistan hosted the First National Seminar on Defense against Biological (and Chemical) Weapons in Karachi. It was organized by the Defense Science and Technology Organization and opened by the then Defense Minister, Aftab Shabaan Mirani.[1] Taking place shortly after Pakistan was pointed at as a country running a productive BW program,[2] this conduct could reflect a Pakistani countermeasure aiming to exhibit, outwardly, adherence to a sheer defensive program.

In September 2001, however, Pakistan did conduct defensive preparations, subsequent to the 9/11 and the concomitant anthrax envelope sabotage acts in the US:

> Scientists and doctors in Pakistan are preparing contingency plans to respond to the threat of biological and other unconventional weapons that could emerge as a result of the crisis in Afghanistan, officials said. As part of the plans, hospital authorities are arranging for extra beds and medicines and are training doctors and paramedical staff in ways to cope in case terrorists unleash such weapons in Pakistan in response to an expected U.S. attack on neighboring Afghanistan. It was thereby noted that Pakistan's two defense laboratories—one in Karachi and the other in Islamabad—were working to prepare enough vaccines to combat anthrax and other biological agents. Pakistan urged the World Health Organization to help Pakistan with technological assistance in preparing a defense against biological weapons.[3]

---

[1] *Saudi Gazette*, 28 April 1995, as cited in 'Chemical Weapons Convention Bulletin', No. 28, June 1995, p. 30.
[2] Collins, Davis, and Bowman, 'Nuclear, Biological, and Chemical Weapon Proliferation: Potential Military Countermeasures', n. 3.
[3] Associated Press, 'Pakistan Gears for Biological Warfare Threat', 30 September 2001, available at http://www.deseretnews.com/article/866529/Pakistangears-for-biological-warfare-threat.html?pg=all, accessed on 12 April 2014.

Notably, one of the steps mentioned was preparing human vaccine against anthrax. An allegation made by Pakistan accused India of using agro-terrorism tactics in 2002 when India offered wheat to Afghanistan. Islamabad claimed that the wheat was infested with seeds of parasitic plants and fungal diseases such as Karnal Bunt, which could affect wheat production. The Government of Pakistan blocked the transportation of grains across its territory since it could harm Pakistani wheat.[1]

Elsewhere, India is described by a Pakistani author as "a career foreign service officer of Pakistan":

The Defense Research and Development Establishment at Gwalior is reportedly working on countering disease threats such as anthrax, brucellosis, cholera, plague, smallpox, viral hemorrhage fever, and botulism.[2]

Reportedly, Pakistan asserted that it is not inclined to produce BW due to the costs involved and the fact that a nuclear weapon state need not go back to outdated techniques and methods of warfare.[3] Such a Pakistani posture ought to be doubted considering a variety of contrasting signs; and that the Pakistani national strategic doctrine at large has been and is considerably affected by the military, both before and after a civilian government was established in 2008.

Connectedly, several review articles published in Pakistan on BW are mostly in favor, technically, of the usefulness and utility of BW, although there is no indication as to whether or not they reflect a crystallized strategic Pakistani approach. The ultimate biological warfare agents (BWAs) mentioned in an

[1] *Standard*, 22 January 2002, cited in Bio-Weapons Monitor 2010, available at: http://www.bwpp.org/documents/BWM%202010%20WEB.pdf, accessed on 12 April 2014.
[2] Ahmed, Zahoor, 'National Implementation of the Biological Weapons Convention—The Case of India and Pakistan', Research Paper No. 34, South Asian Strategic Stability Institute, April 2010, available at http://www.vertic.
[3] Singh, Priyanka, 'Chemical and Biological Weapons: A Case Study of Pakistan', *CBW Magazine*, Vol. 2, No. 3, April–June 2009, pp. 20–23.

article[1] are listed below, in decreasing military usability: small-pox; anthrax; plague; tularemia; botulinum; ricin; gas gangrene; Crimean–Congo hemorrhagic fever; Rift Valley fever; Lassa fever; Ebola hemorrhagic fever; and Marburg disease.

Notably, some of the mentioned pathogens, namely, anthrax, botulinum, gas gangrene and Crimean–Congo hemorrhagic fever, are included within the activities of various facilities in Pakistan. The article concludes: "We know that biological pathogens have been used for biological warfare and terrorism, and their potential for future use is a major concern. Therefore, we must be prepared to respond appropriately if they are used again."[2]

Q fever, a typical BWA, not mentioned earlier, has been elsewhere observed though (in another Pakistani article), to be featured regularly on various threat lists, as it may be considered to be used as a bio-weapon. Therefore, we reviewed the literatures on Q fever to highlight the epidemiologic, economic and public health impact of Q fever as a basis for designing effective control strategies.[3]

A third article on BW was published by the Abbottabad Military Hospital in 2004.[4] Three years after the 9/11 and anthrax sabotage took place in the US, and roughly around the time when the compound occupied by Osama Bin Laden was built in Abbottabad, this article presented a noticeable picture concerning BW. It should be noted that no connection was found between the Abbottabad Military Hospital and the al-Qaeda. Some paragraphs of the review article are worth citing:

According to Dr. Akhter Mohammad, a very senior American public health figure, originally a Pakistani), the use of biological

---

[1] Mansoor, Muhammad Khalid and Lahtasham Khan, 'Biological Weapons: A Threat to Humanity', *The Veterinary News and Views*, Pakistan, 2008, available at http://makepakistanbetter.com/why_how_what_forum.aspx?GroupID=12&ArticleID=5116, accessed on 12 April 2014. Ibid.

[2] Gwida, M., El-Ashker, M. and Khan, I., 'Q Fever: A Re-Emerging Disease?' *Journal of Veterinary Science and Technology*, Vol. 3, No. 5, 2012, p. 120.

[3] Saeed, Waseem and Naseem, Arshad, 'Biological Warfare Agents', *Pakistani Armed Forces Medical Journal*, No. 2, December 2004, available at http://www.pafmj.org/showdetails.php?id=4&t=r, accessed on 12 April 2014.

[4] Ibid.

agents as weapons of mass destruction is no more imaginative, rather it is real. And it is asserted that biological weapons are more destructive and cheaper to produce than chemical weapons, and can certainly be as devastating as nuclear weapons. Unlike chemical agents, who typically lead to violent disease syndromes within minutes at the site of exposure, diseases resulting from biological agents have incubation periods of days; thus delaying the correct diagnosis and appropriate management.

A biological weapon is a device used to intentionally cause disease through dissemination of bacteria, virus or microbial toxin. Depending on the microbe or toxin, resulting disease may or may not be contagious. Biological terrorism, then, is the use of a biological weapon against civilian populations for purposes of creating terror. Generally, the result of use of a biological weapon is an epidemic. The microbial agents required to make some of the biological weapons are widely available, and associated technology is also obtainable, given its legitimate use for agricultural, pharmaceutical or other purposes. Although food, water or insects are potential vehicles for transmission of biological weapons, aerosol dissemination has greatest capacity to cause the disease. According to Dr. Gould, approximately 70 different types of germs can be weaponized for use as agents of biological warfare. The term 'weaponized' refers to packaging or treating an agent so that it becomes easier to distribute to a large area. Potential biological agents include Anthrax, Smallpox, Plague, Botulism, Tularemia, Brucellosis, Viral encephalitis, Staphylococcal enterotoxin B, Viral Hemorrhagic fever (Ebola and Lassa fever viruses), and Q fever.[1]

Skipping anthrax because "in recent times there has been lot of awareness about anthrax as an agent of biological warfare," the cited article does provide a detailed review of smallpox, plague, tularaemia and botulinum as BWAs. A comprehensive article on anthrax was published in 2001 by the Combined Military Hospital, Rawalpindi, together with the Pakistan Air Force Hospital, Islamabad, titled "Anthrax—An Overview in Recent Scenario."[2]

---

[1] Ibid.
[2] Naseem, Arshad, Khan, Badshah, Bhatti, Zulfiqar Ali and Hussain, Iftikhar, 'Anthrax—An Overview in Recent Scenario', *Pakistan Armed*

Handling the Issues of Bioterrorism, Biosecurity and Biosafety

It is fairly evident that collaborative interfaces indeed took place between Pakistani scientists and the al-Qaeda, with the aim of obtaining and weaponizing at least anthrax germs and ricin toxin. Yet, it is unclear whether any of those interfaces was known to any Pakistani at the level of a minister while happening in actuality. Those interfaces formed apparently in the late 1990s and continued into the 2000s.[1] The anthrax envelopes sabotage in the US in September 2001 followed the al-Qaeda 9/11 terror operation and has, in fact, not been deciphered, although in 2008, the Federal Bureau of Investigation (FBI) concluded, ostensibly, that the perpetrator was an American scientist. At any rate, from 2001 to 2008—if not later—the main suspect was al-Qaeda, though it did not have the biotechnological capacity and hence would have needed extraneous professional assistance. Such assistance, if it was lent to al-Qaeda, could originate from Moslem states or Moslem fanatic scientists.

Pakistani authorities indeed took several concrete steps—procedurally at the least—so as to meet the obligations to strengthen controls over sensitive materials and technologies, as set out under United Nations Security Council Resolution 1540. Thus, in September 2004, Pakistan adopted a legislation—the Export Control on Goods, Technologies, Materials and Equipment Related to Biological (and nuclear) Weapons and Their Delivery Systems Act. This Export Control Act was 'to provide for export control on goods, technologies, material and equipment related to nuclear and biological weapons and their delivery systems.[2] The Act has a rigorous mechanism to criminalize and prosecute the individuals and non-state actors involved in the illicit transport of technologies. In addition, in October 2005, Pakistan issued fresh lists of technologies and materials related to the biological (and nuclear) weapons that will be subjected to an intrusive export control system.[3]

Forces Medical Journal, Vol. 51, No. 2, 2001, pp. 153–70.
[1] See http://en.wikipedia.org/wiki/Chaudhry_Abdul_Majeed; *The CBW Conventions Bulletin*: 2006–2009, available at www.sussex.ac.uk/Units/spru/hsp/pdfbulletin.html, accessed on 12 April 2014.
[2] Pakistan—Multilateral Agreements', available at http://ola.iaea.org/factSheets/CountryDetails.asp?country=PK, accessed 19 June 2011
[3] Export Control on Goods, Technologies, Material and Equipment

A comprehensive National Control List (NCL) of various controlled items, based on the Australia Group and further international systems and lists, was issued after a long process (over four years).[1] The NCL can be reviewed and revised at regular intervals or updated and notified accordingly. Pakistan also established the Strategic Export Control Division in 2007, under the Ministry of Foreign Affairs, which would also have an Oversight Board that would independently supervise, tentatively, the implementation of the Export Control Act of 2004 and the other laws/legislations relating to the illicit trafficking and export control mechanisms. Notably, a special body—the 'National Task Force on Biosafety', within the Ministry of Foreign Affairs—was established as well, aiming, in accordance with its title, to consolidate the international image of Pakistan as an obedient state in whatever sense concerned with biotechnologies and pathogens.

Since the mid-2000s, Pakistan has increased its regulation of the biological industry, issuing a set of biosafety rules in 2005 which established a National Biosafety Committee to create guidelines, issue export licenses and inspect facilities dealing with 'living modified organisms or genetically modified organisms'.[2] Also, an updated control list, released in 2011, brought Pakistan's biological export controls in line with those of the Australia Group.[3]

Related to Nuclear and Biological Weapons and their Delivery Systems Act, 2004.

[1] Export Control on Goods, Technologies, Material and Equipment Related to Nuclear and Biological Weapons and their Delivery Systems Act, 2004, November 2004, available at www.iaea.org/Publications/Documents/Infcircs/2004/infcirc636.pdf, accessed 19 June 2011.

[2] Khan, Zulfqar, 'Safeguards against Illicit Transfers: Pakistan's Institutional Response', Brussels, Belgium, 16–17 November 2006, available at www. sassi.org/.../Brussels%20conference%20on%20illicit%20 transfers%20 %20November%202006.pdf, accessed on 22 June 2011. Pakistan Environmental Protection Agency, 'Pakistan Biosafety Rules, 2005: Notification', S.R.O. (I) 336(I)/2005, 21 April 2005, available at www. environment.gov.pk, accessed on 12 April 2014.

[3] Communication of 17 October 2011 from the Permanent Mission of Pakistan to the Agency Concerning the Export Control Policies of the Government of Pakistan and a Statutory Regulatory Order, INFCIRC/832, 30 November 2011, available at www.iaea.org, accessed on 12 April 2014.

The year 2011 marked two Pakistani articles on biosafety and biosecurity in Pakistan, delivered from the Armed Forces Institute of Pathology and the National Commission on Biotechnology, Ministry of Science and Technology. The two articles emphasize the various actions taken by Pakistan, compatibly with bio-risk managements. The article provided by the Armed Forces Institute of Pathology[1] is more informative then the other one[2] and contains details about: the National Biosafety Committee; the National Core Group in Life Sciences; and the Biological Safety Association.

Interestingly, the second article, albeit less informative, adds to the list two universities: Aga Khan University; and Quaid-i-Azam University. The two universities are thereby mentioned within the context of developing a National Biosafety Centre and an operating project that includes the elements of bioethics, biosecurity and dual use, namely, 'Engagement and Awareness Rising on Bioethics, Biosecurity and Dual-Use Education Project 2011–2012.

Noticeably, in February 2012, the Pakistani PM reportedly received a postal package containing anthrax spores (details in the next section). The event certainly amplified an ongoing Pakistani effort taking place for about a decade already, in the related fields of bio-preparedness, biosecurity and biosafety, altogether. Although there is such a genuine effort in Pakistan, at the same time, it considerably serves for strengthening a Pakistani façade— that of a country that is fully committed and entirely follows in reality its undertakings in those respects as well as in tangential respects related to the BWC, ostensibly. However, practically, it also facilitates the acquisition of biohazard instrumentation that can support, technically, BW development and production taking place in parallel within certain Pakistani installations.

---

[1] Improving Implementation of the Biological Weapons Convention – Case Study I: Biosafety and Biosecurity in Pakistan, United Nations Institute for Disarmament Research, 2011, available at http://www.isn.ethz.ch/Digital-Library/Publications/Detail/?ots591=0c54e3b3-1e9c-bele-2c24-a6a8c7060233&lng=en&id=134406, accessed on 12 April 2014.

[2] Civil Society Preparations for the 7th BWC Review Conference 2011', available at http://www.bwpp.org/revcon-education.html.

Bio-protection-related Facilities, Pakistan Council of Scientific and Industrial Research

Affiliated with the Ministry of Science and Technology, this Council reportedly received from the Pakistani PM's office the anthrax-containing parcel sent to the Pakistani PM in 2012 in order to look into it.[1] Another report noted that the parcel had been submitted to this Council by an unidentified intelligence agency, and then sent to a facility in Lahore for scientific analysis. It was reported that 'The laboratory tests have proven presence of anthrax spores in the parcel and it has been handed over to the agency with results.[2] A facility located in Lahore is the Council's Food and Biotechnology Research Centre, which has a bacteriological laboratory. The latter holds regular pathogenic bacteria, including Salmonella typhi, multi-drug resistant Pseudomonas aeruginosa and enterohaemorrhagic Escherichia coli.[3] Two additional facilities affiliated with the Council are located elsewhere: the Environmental Analytical Laboratory in Islamabad[4] and the Pharmaceutical Research Centre in Karachi.[5] Considering that the identification of the anthrax germs contained in the parcel sent to the Pakistani PM took place in a facility of the Council, it would appear as if it is the Council which has such national responsibility. Beyond that, however, no exceptional activities could be traced in the facilities affiliated with the Council.

[1] Singh, Gunjan, 'Anthrax Threat in Pakistan—Global Context and Regional Consequences', *CBW Magazine*, Vol. 5, No. 1, January–June 2012, pp. 23-25.
[2] See 'Pakistani Lab Could Take another Look at Anthrax Package', *Pakistan Today*, 3 February 2012, available at available at http://www.nti.org/gsn/article/pakistani-police-take-another-look-anthrax-package/, accessed on 12 April 2014.
[3] Hassan, Ammara, Rahman, Salma, Deeba, Farah and Mahmud, Shahid, 'Antimicrobial Activity of Some Plant Extracts having Hepatoprotective Effects', *Journal of Medicinal Plant Research*, Vol. 3, No. 1, 2009, pp. 20–23.
[4] Batool, Syeda Afifa, Kalsoom, Razia, Rauf, Naseem, Tahir, S.S. and Hussain, Fouzia, 'Microbial and Physico-chemical Quality Assessment of the Raw and Pasteurized Milk Supplied in the Locality of Twin City of Pakistan', Internet Journal of Food Safety, Vol. 14, 2012, pp. 17–22.
[5] Saleem, M., Rehman, A. and Afza, N., 'Efficacy of 0.3% Topical Ciprofloxacin and Tobramycin of Ophthalmic Solutions in the Treatment of Experimental Pseudamonas Aeruginosa Keratitis in Rabbits', *Pakistan Journal of Medical Research*, Vol. 47, No. 2, 2008, pp. 37–39.

National Institute of Health

Two hundred thirty suspicious samples were received by the institute from November 2001 to March 2002, and these were analyzed for anthrax. Detailed procedures applied by the institute for that specific purpose are presented in an eight-pages paper published in 2004.[1] While the institute has been widely involved in monitoring possible anthrax sabotage, such monitoring was taken care of by the Pakistan Council of Scientific and Industrial Research, later on, in the case of the parcel sent to the Pakistani PM (as detailed above). In the Biological Production Division of the National Institute of Health, industrial cultivation of the pathogens of typhoid, cholera, Cl. tetani (toxoid) and viral pathogens (rabies, measles) takes place, for manufacturing the respective vaccines.[2]

National Veterinary Institute

In the National Veterinary Institute (Veterinary Research Institute, Lahore), reportedly 18 different bacterial and viral vaccines are produced, mostly unspecified. Details are available concerning vaccines against anthrax and various Clostridia (plus toxoids).[3] A viral vaccine—foot-and-mouth disease (FMD)—has been produced too, and, as of 2008, was reported to be of poor quality; however, in 2008 and 2009, vaccines against two other viral diseases—ovine rinderpest and highly pathogenic H5N1 avian influenza—were judged successful.[4]

Certainly constituting a cardinal and legitimate component of the Pakistani biomedical infrastructure in general, and bearing distinct (yet unimplemented, as far as could be seen) ability to support BWA production on an industrial scale, those two vaccine-producing institutes— the National Institute of Health

---

[1] Available at http://applications.emro.who.int/emhj/1001_2/emhj_2004_10_1_2_19_26.pdf, accessed on 12 April 2014.

[2] Available at http://www.nih.org.pk/Bio_Prod.asp, accessed on 12 April 2014.

[3] Available at http://www.icpsr.org.ma/?Page=showInstitute&InstituteID=VR I2342&CountryID=pakistan, accessed on 12 April 2014.

[4] Asim, M., Rashid, A., Chaudhary, A.H. and Noor, M.S., 'Production of Homologous Live Attenuated Cell Culture Vaccine for the Control of Peste des Petits Ruminants in Small Ruminants', *Pakistan Veterinary Journal*, Vol.

and the National Veterinary Institute—apparently have the capacity to handle and store highly virulent pathogens.

Biological Safety Level-3 (BSL-3) Facilities

At the basic biomedical infrastructure level, the situation is that a common human pathogen, the tuberculosis bacterium, which is widely explored in Pakistan, requires a BSL-3 facility. The National Tuberculosis Programme of Pakistan planned the upgrading of five BSL-3 facilities (plus 16 BSL-2); though it is not clear to what extent this program has been implemented thus far. Specifically, BSL-3 facilities for handling tuberculosis were reported to exist at the Aga Khan University and the Indus Hospital, Karachi. Two additional tentative/in effect BSL-3 facilities include: a world-class BSL-3 tuberculosis laboratory as part of the KfW-funded 'Tuberculosis Control Programme in Khyber Pakhtunkhwa' project; and a BSL-3 tuberculosis laboratory in Punjab at Al Razi Healthcare.[1] Further tentative/in effect BSL-3 facilities include: a bioreactor in a modular BSL-3 facility for the industrial production of rabies vaccine in the National Institute of Health;[2] and a BSL-3 facility for handling highly pathogenic avian influenza H5N1 viruses.[3] A vaccine manufacturing facility of In Vitro Vogue Pvt Ltd is intended to be 'Pakistan's first state of the art BSL-3 animal vaccine manufacturing facility', and is to be established at the Lahore Biotech Park, located on the Barki Road, Lahore, for the University of Veterinary and Animal Sciences of Lahore.[4]

The equipment and know-how found in the mentioned vaccine production facilities enable, technically, serial production of anthrax, botulinum, Cl. perfringens (bacterium plus toxins),

---

[1] No. 2, 2009, pp. 72–74; Iqbal, M., Nisar, M., Anwarul-Haq, Noor, S.and Gill, Z.J., 'Evaluation of Oil Based Avian Influenza Vaccine (H5NI) Prepared with Different Concentrations of Adjuvant', *Pakistan Veterinary Journal*, Vol. 28, No. 4, 2008, pp. 205–06. Available at www.lifehealthonline.com/tip/al-razi-healthcare.../DBEqZ7u0IX8.html.
[2] http://www.pakmissionuk.gov.pk/commsection/london/invest_opportunities/Establishment_of_Cell_revised_21.1.2010.pdf
[3] Pakistan and FAO Achievements and success stories, May 2011, published by FAO Representation in Pakistan, available at http://www.fao.org/fileadmin/templates/rap/files/epublications/PakistanedocFINAL.pdf.
[4] Available at http://www.invitrovogue.com/contact.html.

Salmonella, V. cholera, and probably certain viruses, for military purposes. However, there are no indications that such production has thus far been conducted in those facilities. The know-how can be utilized, though, elsewhere in Pakistan. It appears that Pakistan is presently self-competent in terms of meeting its needs up to the level of BSL-3 facilities.

It is of note that, in actuality, there are still gaps between required and in effect biosafety measures in Pakistan, as is, for example, the typical case with tuberculosis, a common pathogen in Pakistan that has to be handled under BSL-3 conditions. Nevertheless, this may indicate, indirectly, that Pakistani labs included in or supporting a BW program could likely hold and handle in BSL-2 facilities those pathogens that require BSL-3, and in BSL-3 facilities those pathogens that require BSL-4. In such case, even if a BSL-4 facility is not found in Pakistan, most infectious and virulent pathogens might be handled and stored in Pakistan.

Suspected BW Facilities

While it is not clear whether the above-mentioned facilities are involved in a Pakistani BW program, sanctions were imposed on four other facilities that were suspected to be involved. In 1998, the US imposed sanctions (which were later on lifted, in 2001) on four Pakistani entities on the suspicion that they could be involved in biological (and chemical) weapons activities, namely: (i) the National Institute of Biotechnology and Genetic Engineering (NIBGE), Faisalabad; (ii) the Centre for Advanced Molecular Biology, Lahore; (iii) Chemical and Biological Weapons Research Institute (at the University of Karachi's Husein Ebrahim Jamal Research Institute of Chemistry); and (iv) Chemical and Biological Warfare Research and Development Laboratory (part of the official Defense Science and Technology Organization).[1] The third and fourth facilities consequently became non-existent, whereas the first and second still persist.

---

[1] Rules and Regulations', Federal Register, Vol. 63, No. 223, 19 November 1998, available at http://frwebgate.access.gpo.gov/cgi-oc.cgi?dbname=.

National Institute for Biotechnology and Genetic Engineering, Faisalabad

Primarily affiliated with the PAEC, the institute contains a Health Biotechnology Division, which specialized, indirectly, on a *Clostridium botulinum* toxin (botulinolysin), from 1992 until 1998 (and probably later). From 1999 onwards, no more works were published in that field. A shift to the enteric bacterial pathogens, Salmonella, Shigella, Klebsiella and E. coli, including Shigella toxin, took place (as far as reflected in published works). Genetic factors responsible for virulence, toxinogenicity and broad resistance to drugs were investigated. The enteric viral pathogen, rotavirus, was investigated as well. Two notable pathogens investigated in another division of the institute—the Environmental Biotechnology Division—was Brucella abortus and FMD virus.[1] In 2007, rinderpest samples (spleen, lungs, liver, lymphoid tissue and occulo-nasal swabs) from cattle and buffalos, collected from 1985–94 and kept at −70ºC in the institute, were molecularly diagnosed for rinderpest.[2]

Also, the institute was involved in isolating the highly pathogenic avian influenza virus, H5N1, in Pakistan.[3] It was involved in studying the virulence of the fungal wheat pathogens, Puccinia striiformis[4] and Puccinia triticina[5] as well. Collectively, the

[1] Asif, M., Ali, R.A., Masroor, E.B., Ahmad, A., Sehrish, F. and Khan, Q.M., 'Development of Genetic Marker for Molecular Detection of Brucella Abortus', *Pakistan Journal of Zoology*, Vol. 9, 2009, pp. 267–71; Waheed, U., Saeed, A., Ameena, M. and Khan, Q.M., 'The Vp1 (Capsid Protein) Gene Based DNA Sequencing for Epidemiological Analysis of FMDV Isolated from Buffaloes in Pakistan', *Pakistan Journal of Zoology*, Vol. 9, 2009, pp. 333–39.

[2] Farooq, U., Khan, Q. Mahmood, and Barrett, T., 'Molecular Diagnosis of Rinderpest and Peste des Petits Ruminants Virus using Trizol Reagent',*Pakistan Veterinary Journal*, Vol. 28, No. 2, 2008, pp. 63–67.

[3] Saeed, A., Afzal, F., Arshad, M., Hassan, S. and Abubakar, M., 'Detection of Avian Influenza Virus H5N1 Serotype in Backyard Poultry, Wild and Zoo Birds in Pakistan', *Revue Méd. Vét.*, Vol. 163, No. 11, 2012, pp. 552–57.

[4] Bux, Hadi, Rasheed, Awais, Siyal, Mahboob Ali, Kazi, Alvina G., Napar, Abdul Aziz and Mujeeb-Kazi, A., 'An Overview of Stripe Rust of Wheat (Puccinia striiformis f. sp. tritici) in Pakistan', *Archives of Phytopathology and Plant Protection*, Vol. 45, No. 19, 2012, pp. 2278–89.

[5] Fayyaz, M., Rattu, A.R., Ahmad, I., Akhtar, M.A., Hakro, A.A. and Mujeeb- Kazi, A., 'Current Status of the Occurrence and Distribution of (Puccinia triticina) Wheat Leaf Rust Virulence in Pakistan', *Pakistan Journal of Botany*, Vol. 40, No. 2, 2008, pp. 887–95.

published activities of the institute seem to have changed consequent to the 1998 American sanctions. Besides, originally under the auspices of the PAEC, the affiliation of the institute was changed, reportedly becoming the Pakistan Institute/University of Engineering and Applied Sciences, Nilore, Islamabad.[1]

The latter appears to be affiliated with the Pakistan Engineering Council and with the Higher Education Commission of Pakistan. Certain labs in the NIGEBE probably continue to deal with BWAs, particularly Clostridial toxins plus enteropathogens, and master applicable know-how regarding any botulinum toxin. Dealing with the pathogens causing brucellosis, rinderpest, FMD and H5N1 influenza is regarded to be significant as well, in terms of potential BWAs. Notable too is the involvement of the institute in studies on the virulence, under field conditions, of fungal pathogens causing wheat stripe rust and wheat leaf rust, known as potential BWAs.

Centre for Advanced Molecular Biology

Largely diversified scientific activities—of which appreciable portions may potentially relate to BWAs—are identified with the centre:[2]

1. Pox virus—preparation and evaluation of buffalo pox virus vaccine.
2. Pasteurella—usage of Pasteurella mullocida dense culture for vaccine preparation.
3. Bacillus—a variety of aspects regarding Bacillus thuringiensis (basically as bioinsecticide).
4. Plasmid-mediated antibiotic resistance in Shigella and Pseudomonas.
5. Various aspects pertaining to Brucella, Klebsiella, Vibrio cholera and Salmonella.
6. Plasmodium falciparum (combinatorial metabolism).
7. Modification of a malaria vaccine.

---

[1] Habeeb, M.A., Haque, A., Nematzadeh, S., Iversen, A. and Giske, C.G.,'High Prevalence of 16S rRNA Methylase RmtB among CTX-M Extendedspectrum b-lactamase-producing Klebsiella Pneumoniae from Islamabad, Pakistan', International Journal of Antimicrobial Agents, Vol. 41, No. 6, 2013, pp. 524–26.
[2] Available at http://zsp.com.pk/CV.pdf

8. Cloning of viral genes (hepatitis B virus) into a high expression vector pKk223-3.

9. Bacteriophages

The centre was founded within the Punjab University by the Ministry of Science and Technology in 1987. It has interfaces with an unaffiliated facility named Institute of Molecular Sciences and Bioinformatics, Lahore as well as with the related Punjab University-affiliated Centre of Excellence in Molecular Biology.[1] One notable work published by the latter is on isolation and genotypic characterization of new hepatitis E viruses.[2]

The remarkable range of pathogens and aspects dealt within the Centre for Advanced Molecular Biology fits its involvement in BW-oriented research, development and production, and may account—at the level of open information, at the least—for the institute being sanctioned. A considerable part of the BW-oriented work might rely on model pathogens, such as pox virus and Bacillus. Alongside, other pathogens dealt with like Brucella, Klebsiella pneumoniae and Vibrio cholerae are employable as BWAs.

Foreign Intelligence and Academic Assessments

Beyond, and in contrast with, the obedient profile fostered by Pakistan as a state party to the BWC, there are assessments, if not concrete intelligence, which point out the opposite: that Pakistan does run a BW program and has been doing so for already more than 20 years. Following is a synopsis in that regard. In a 1992 DIA document released under the Freedom of Information Act, Pakistan is mentioned as a country believed to have launched a BW program.[3] A study prepared in 1994 for the US Congress on potential military countermeasures against nucle-

---

[1] Available at http://www.cemb.edu.pk/intro.html

[2] Iqbal, Tahir, Idrees, Muhammad, Ali, Liaqat, Hussain, Abrar, Ali, Muhammad, Butt, Sadia, Yousaf, Muhammad Zubair and Sabar, Muhammad Farooq, 'Isolation and Characterization of Two New Hepatitis E Virus Genotype 1 Strains from Two Mini-outbreaks in Lahore, Pakistan', *Virology Journal*, Vol. 8, No. 94, 2011, available at http://www.virologyj.com/content/8/1/94.

[3] 'Proliferation of WMD', DIA Document DST-2660-694-92, May 1992. 53. Collins, Davis and Bowman, 'Nuclear, Biological, and Chemical Weapon Proliferation: Potential Military Countermeasures', n. 3.

ar and chemical–biological weapons proliferation categorized Pakistan with respect to BW as 'probable possessor', while one degree of lower ranking is 'suspected (BW) program' and the higher (actually the highest) degree is 'possession confirmed' (Russia only).[1]

The same year, Pakistan was mentioned in Germany as a country 'on the point of establishing its own production of BW', according to a quote from a confidential BND report.[2] Two years later, a US Department of Defense report noted that Pakistan was 'conducting research and development with potential biological warfare applications.[3]

As mentioned earlier, in 1998, the US imposed sanctions on four Pakistani entities on the suspicion that they could be involved in biological (and chemical) weapons activities. The Canadian Security Intelligence Service estimated Pakistan to be a country 'of greatest concern from a proliferation perspective', in a report on BW proliferation, issued in 2000.[4]

Beyond being 'active in the area of defensive biological (and chemical) weapons research', as assessed by the German Federal Customs Administration, 'Pakistan's monetary expenditure for its nuclear and missile programs leaves little scope for it to mount an offensive biological (and chemical) weapon programs, though this cannot be proved'.[5] Certainly improvable, the latter equation-like observation is at any rate doubtful.

Moreover, it has elsewhere been assessed that Pakistan would likely 'invest in offensive weapons, because its infantry forces are outnumbered five to one and outgunned three to one in tanks and artillery when compared with Indian forces.' Biological (and chemical) weapons might thus be needed, according to

[1] Death and Terror from the Laboratory', *Der Spiegel* (Hamburg), 22 August 1994, pp. 22-25.
[2] Available at http://www.csis-scrs.gc.ca/pblctns/prspctvs/200005-eng.asp 1996
[3] Canadian Security Intelligence Service (CSIS), 'Biological Weapons Proliferation', prepared and published by CSIS, 9 June 2000, available at https://www.csis-scrs.gc.ca/pblctns/prspctvs/200005-eng.asp.
[4] German Federal Customs Administration, The Export Controls: Information about Countries of Concern, November 2004, available at www. zollkriminalamt.de
[5] Mauroni, Albert J., *Chemical and Biological Warfare: A Reference Handbook*, California: ABC-CLIO Inc., 2007, pp. 76-77.

the Pakistani concept, since nuclear weapons do not help in the numerous smaller conflicts that continue to occur between the two nations. Pakistan may see biological (and chemical) weapons as the way to counter the larger Indian forces, much as Iraq held off superior Iranian numbers in their conflict.[1]

Indirectly, yet relevantly, it has further been observed that in case two Third World states become bogged down in attrition warfare, there might be a temptation to use BW against the enemy's front line forces, if only to cause logistic and morale problems.[2] Pakistan might conceivably follow such a line. Another study, issued by the European Union (EU) Non-Proliferation Consortium, contended that Pakistan would 'on paper, be well placed to produce biological (and chemical) warfare agents', although 'there is no evidence of any active Pakistani program in the areas of offensive biological (or chemical) warfare.[3]

Eventually, the US Congress set an action stating: 'US President must make securing biological (and nuclear) materials and weapons in Pakistan a priority. Congress should ensure that sufficient funding is authorized and appropriated for this purpose.[4]

It is of note that Pakistan has been repeatedly regarded to be one of several countries illegitimately possessing the smallpox virus (which is internationally disallowed, except for the US and Russia). In that connection, from 1970 to 1972, extensive

---

[1] Zilinskas, Raymond A., 'Biological Warfare and the Third World', Politics and the Life Sciences, Vol. 9, No. 1, August 1990, pp. 59–76.
[2] . Tetrais, Bruno, 'Pakistan's Nuclear and WMD Programmes: Status, Evolution and Risks', EU Non-Proliferation Consortium, Non-Proliferation Paper No. 19, July 2012.
[3] Available at http://www.foxnews.com/story/2008/12/02/nuclear-or-bioterror-attack-on-us-likely-by-2013-panel-warns/#ixzz2e6BAzMfS.
[4] Heiner, Gordon G., Nusrat Fatima, Richard W. Daniel, June L. Cole, Ronald L. Anthony and Fred R. McCrumb, 'A Study of Inapparent Infection in Smallpox', 1971, available at http://apps.who.int/iris/ bitstream/10665/67484/1/WHO_SE_71.26.pdf; Heiner, G.G., Fatima, N. and McCrumb, Jr, F.R., 'A Study of Intrafamilial Transmission of Smallpox', *American Journal of Epidemiology*, Vol. 94, No. 4, 1971, pp. 316–26; David B. Thomas, William M. McCormace, Isao Arita, Malik Muzaffer Khan, Shafiqul Islam ad Thomas M. Mack, 'Endemic Smallpox in Rural East Pakistan', 1971, available at http://whqlibdoc.who.int/ smallpox/WHO_SE_71.24.pdf; Mack, T.M., Thomas, D.B. and Khan, M.M., 'Epidemiology of Smallpox in West Pakistan: Determinants of Intravillage Spread Other than Acquired Immunity, American Journal of Epidemiology, Vol. 95, 1972, pp. 157–68.

field studies on smallpox outbreaks that occurred in Pakistan took place (some publications are referred to in that respect). It can be assumed, then, that the virus was actually isolated, and in that case, the virus might be held in Pakistan until present.

Conclusions

Collectively, taking into account the above-mentioned observations, there is apparently a sound rationale which led Pakistan to pursue BW and establish a strategic concept in accordance. The various considerations and postulations underlying a presumed Pakistani seeking for BW, as described herein, are regarded to be plausible. It can be concluded that an active BW program, in all likelihood, commenced in Pakistan in the 1980s. It possibly yielded a first-generation BW arsenal by 1994. Otherwise, a first-generation BW arsenal probably came into being during the second half of the 1990s or the first half of the 2000s.

The timing of the sanctions imposed by the US on the Pakistani biological entities—in 1998—was rather in the wake of Pakistan's May 1998 nuclear tests, when the US Department of Commerce imposed sanctions on a large number of government and quasi-government entities. However, the case, in terms of an apparent Pakistani active BW program, was already there.

Although it is publicly accentuated that an ongoing Pakistani BW program cannot be proved, it is fairly clear that some Western intelligence agencies possess classified information which is highly supportive of such an active program taking place in actuality. The biotechnological and biomedical infrastructures of Pakistan evidently enable such a program. Ongoing development and upgrading have been observed connectedly, underlying a significant Pakistani sub-nuclear weapon of mass destruction capability.

Acknowledgements

Courtesy: *Journal of Defense Studies*, India Vol. 8, No. 2, April–June 2014.

(This last chapter is taken with special permission of Mr. Dany Shoham, from his article "Pakistan and Biological Weapons," *Jour-

nal of Defense Studies, Vol. 8, No. 2, April–June 2014, pp. 85-108, online at http://idsa.in/jds/8_2_2014_PakistanandBiologicalWeapons.

Mr. Shoham works with the Begin–Sadat Center for Strategic Studies, Bar Ilan University, Israel. He was until recently a Visiting Fellow at the Institute for Defense Studies and Analyses (IDSA), New Delhi. Moreover, the author wishes to express his appreciation to Brig. Rumel Dahiya (Retd.), Deputy Director General of IDSA, and to Dr. Ajey Lele, Head of Strategic Technologies Research Centre at IDSA, for supporting this study.)

POSTSCRIPT

During the last three years, the threat of nuclear, biological and chemical terrorism in the European Union prompted many changes in security infrastructure and law enforcement mechanism. The current security crisis, lake of mutual trust and security sector reforms further increased in their inner pain. The European Union lacks the competence to bring about the necessary harmonization of the national economies whose levels of competitiveness are drifting far apart. The project is unprepared for a terrorist attack using biological weapons. In Dec 2002, the member states adopted a joint program on CBRN: chemical, biological and radiological and nuclear risks to strengthen risk assessment, and reduce risk to population, the environment, food chain through protective measures. Another effort of the EU was strict surveillance to detect airborne chemical agents.

On 23 June 2016, with the Brexit from the EU, the whole infrastructure of intelligence cooperation on law enforcement between the United Kingdom and the EU came under serious threat. The UK citizens voted to leave the project, while European leadership issued conflagrated statement, hammering the UK leadership for its unexpected decision. French President François Hollande said Britain's vote seriously challenged the EU, and that the union must focus on key priorities like security and defense, border protection and job creation. "The British vote is a tough test for Europe," Hollande said in a televised address. German Chancellor Angela Merkel said the European Union is strong enough to find the "right answers" to Britain's vote to leave the bloc.

On 24 June 2016, the European Union leaders reacted with disappointment to the Brexit news but expressed determination to maintain the bloc's unity. European Commission President Jean-Claude Juncker urged not to consider Brexit the beginning of the end of the EU, while European Council President Donald Tusk said, "What doesn't kill you, makes you stronger". The United Kingdom's exit from the EU was expected to take at least two years. Tusk and other EU leaders urged London to give effect to its decision to leave the bloc as soon as possible. "We now expect the United Kingdom government to give effect to this decision of the British people as soon as possible, however, painful that process may be. Any delay would unnecessarily prolong uncertainty," said the statement, signed by Tusk, Juncker, as well as EU Parliament President Martin Schulz and EU Council Presidency holder and Dutch Prime Minister Mark Rutte. The NATO Secretary General Jens Stoltenberg said Brexit has shown the growing role of the alliance in the new realities. "Today, as we face more instability and uncertainty, NATO is more important than ever as a platform for cooperation among European allies, and between Europe and North America," said Stoltenberg.

Russian President Vladimir Putin said the Brexit vote reflects discontent of the British people with the state of security and their unwillingness to subsidize weaker economies. "I believe it is clear for ordinary British subjects why it occurred," Mr. Putin said. The UN Secretary General Ban Ki-moon said he expects the UK and EU to remain solid partners for the United Nations. "The Secretary-General expects the European Union to continue to be a solid partner for the United Nations on development and humanitarian issues, as well as peace and security, including migration," Ban Ki-moon said in a statement. The Brexit created new tensions; Professor of Law Sionaidh Douglas-Scott at Queen Mary University of London said: "There is no cast-iron guarantee on acquired rights in the event Britain leaves the EU. If you leave the EU you are no longer a member of the club that gives you those rights."

On the financial front, the global stock markets including those based in London, New York, Mumbai, Karachi, Hong Kong and Tokyo plummeted, and 200 billion sterling pounds were wiped off in just a few hours from London's FTSE Stock Exchange alone. The referendum's result also crashed the sterling pound against other currencies with an all time low figure against the dollar since 1985. Some viewed the vote on Brexit as the triumph of xenophobic forces in Britain along with its narrow brand of nationalism. This was because the EU was a project that aimed at regional integration, and transcending the artificial barriers created by the dominance of nationalism. The British voters rejected the bid to remain in the UK on renegotiated terms. This was a great blow to the EU and set a precedent for other members to follow suit, along with the practice of renegotiating terms of membership. For the UK, Brexit raised more questions than it answered.

The UK left for 10 reasons including; freedom to make stronger trade deals with other nations, freedom to spend UK resources presently through EU membership in the UK to the advantage of our citizens, freedom to control our national borders, freedom to restore Britain's special legal system, freedom to deregulate the EU's costly mass of laws, freedom to make major savings for British consumers, freedom to improve the British economy and generate more jobs, freedom to regenerate Britain's fisheries, freedom to save the NHS from EU threats to undermine it by harmonizing healthcare across the EU, and to reduce welfare payments to non-UK EU citizens, and freedom to restore British customs and traditions.

Cases of nuclear smuggling in some European states indicate that the possibilities of the use of nuclear, chemical and biological weapons cannot be ruled out. In Europe, there is the general perception that as extremist and sectarian groups have already used some dangerous gases in Iraq, Afghanistan and Syria, therefore, they could use biological weapons against civilian populations in Europe. If control over these weapons is weak, or if their components are available in the open market, terrorists can inflict huge fatalities in the region. Experts recently warned that the availability of such materials in the open markets of some European states can fall in the hands of local terrorist organizations, which may further jeopardize the security of the region.

Two Belgian nuclear power plant workers had joined ISIS, leading to fears that jihadists had the intelligence to cause a meltdown disaster. Before the suicide attacks in Belgium, security agencies were fearful that perhaps ISIS operatives had been looking to target a nuclear plant as it emerged that two workers from a plant in Doel fled to Syria to join ISIS. Belgian Interior Minister Jan Jambon said at the time that authorities had determined there was a threat "to the person in question, but not the nuclear facilities."

The threat of nuclear terrorism and the use of dirty bomb by terrorist organizations in Britain and Europe cannot be ruled out as these groups have established close relationships with some disgruntled elements within government circles. They have established strong contacts with foreign embassies and terrorist organizations across the borders. The threat is very real, but some irresponsible states do not realize the sensitivity of the situation. The changing nature of the threat and the dramatic rise of the ISIS is a matter of great concern for major nuclear powers in Europe.

Despite the above-mentioned vulnerabilities, experts warned that Taliban, extremist groups and the ISIS are capable of acquiring and deploying a mass-casualty biological weapon, and are likely to develop more capability in the near future. Some of them argue that the process of turning a bacterium or a virus into a weapon is technically very difficult. Therefore even if a bioterrorism attack happens, it is likely to use a 'sub-optimal' pathogen disseminated through crude delivery methods and therefore have only limited impact. Bioterrorism is the intentional release of harmful biological agents such as bacteria, viruses, or toxins. To protect citizens and national infrastructure, the race is on to improve Europe's preparedness. For terrorist organizations like the Islamic State, London, Paris, Brussels and Amsterdam are the number one target of bio-terrorists.

The last three decades witnessed a significant rise in the profile of nuclear, radiological, chemical and biological terrorism. With the test of Pakistan's nuclear weapons in May 1998, International community put the threat of nuclear terrorism in South Asia at the forefront of its security agenda. Now, as the United States and its allies focus intensely on the nuclear developments in North Korea and Iran, the distraction of international community on the danger of India and Pakistan's nuclear and biological weapons has put the security and stability of the subcontinent at spike. Notwithstanding the US recent pressure on Pakistan to stop making dangerous weapons, the army rejected and said it was a matter of the country's national security.

As the world has entered the era of mass murder techniques, ISIS and Takfiri terrorist organizations in Britain and Europe are trying to retrieve materials of dirty bomb and inflict maximum possible carnage to achieve their goal. Making a crude bomb for them is not a difficult task as highly professional and technical people have joined their ranks. International press reports on insufficient security dynamics of nuclear materials in Europe, but international community does not seek improvement of security of their nuclear installations. Despite some progress over the past decades, the security of nuclear weapons is endangered, as some materials remain dangerously vulnerable to theft. Pakistan and India also continue to expand their nuclear arsenals, now numbering many hundreds, and continue to rely on doctrines likely to lead to early dispersal of those weapons in the event of a crisis.

In 2006, former Chief Minister of Baluchistan, Akhtar Mengal claimed that Pakistan army used chemical weapons against the people of Baluchistan. He, however, showed pictures of Bloch civilians who had been hit by these weapons. Mr. Mengal demanded the presence of international mediators to oversight the ongoing conflict in the province. "Chemical weapons are being used and large number of women, and children died", Mengal said. Mr. Mengal revelations were supported by the Human Rights Commission of Pakistan (HRCP). The recent attacks on nuclear facilities, combined with the country's political and economic instability, and history of supporting non state actors in India and Afghanistan, has long made it a potential nuclear terrorism threat. The November 13, 2015 terrorist attacks in France and the March 2016 attacks in Brussels, in which terrorists sought to retrieve nuclear weapons raised serious question about the nuclear security of EU member states. In several EU member states, experts of improvised explosives and nuclear explosives have reportedly come from Pakistan, Afghanistan, Africa and the Arab world.

Terrorists could attack or sabotage nuclear facilities, such as commercial nuclear power plants or research reactors, to cause a release of radioactive elements. On April 1, 2016, The Telegraph reported that the British prime minister warned that ISIS was planning to use drones to spray nuclear materials over Western cities. A British official told newspapers that world leaders already fear that the ISIS is trying to get nuclear, chemical and biological weapons to use them against civilians and nuclear installation in Europe. The possible risks of terrorists gaining access to the country's HEU stockpile assumes more dangerous proportion with the current state of political instability in Pakistan headed by a weak government. However, these assumptions should be validated before drawing any conclusion on the potential threat of nuclear terrorism emanating from Pakistan.

The Brussels terrorist attacks proved the competency of the ISIS to infiltrate into the nuclear infrastructure of the country where two nuclear experts joined the group. The same is possible in Pakistan where the ISIS network recruits people from all section of society. International community has longstanding worries about the purported radicalization of the armed forces of Pakistan, fearing that extremist elements within the army may possibly facilitate the TTP, ISIS or other extremist groups to carryout terrorist attacks against the nuclear installations of the country. Recent reports in Pakistan warned that the greatest threat of nuclear terrorism is inevitable as the loose of nuclear material by insiders entered at crucial phase. However, the Britain's withdrawal from the European needs to invoke Article 50 of the 1992 Maastricht Treaty on European Union.

Article 50 of the 1992 Maastricht Treaty on European Union

1. Any Member State may decide to withdraw from the Union in accordance with its own constitutional requirements.

2. A Member State which decides to withdraw shall notify the European Council of its intention. In the light of the guidelines provided by the European Council, the Union shall negotiate and conclude an agreement with that State, setting out the arrangements for its withdrawal, taking account of the framework for its future relationship with the Union. That agreement shall be negotiated in accordance with Article 218(3) of the Treaty on the Functioning of the European Union. It shall be concluded on behalf of the Union by the Council, acting by a qualified majority, after obtaining the consent of the European Parliament.

3. The Treaties shall cease to apply to the State in question from the date of entry into force of the withdrawal agreement or, failing that, two years after the notification referred to in paragraph 2, unless the European Council, in agreement with the Member State concerned, unanimously decides to extend this period.

4. For the purposes of paragraphs 2 and 3, the member of the European Council or of the Council representing the withdrawing Member State shall not participate in the discussions of the European Council or Councilor in decisions concerning it.

   A qualified majority shall be defined in accordance with Article 238(3) (b) of the Treaty on the Functioning of the European Union.

5. If a State which has withdrawn from the Union asks to rejoin, its request shall be subject to the procedure referred to in Article 49.

Consolidated versions of the Treaty on European Union and the Treaty on the Functioning of the European Union 2012/C 326/01, (Courtesy: Open Europe 2016).

BIBLIOGRAPHY

Acton, James M. 2014, International Verification and Intelligence, *Intelligence and National Security journal, Vol. 29*

Aid, Matthew M, 2003, All Glory is Fleeting: Sigint and the Fight against International Terrorism, *Intelligence and National Security journal, Vol. 18*

Akkad O. 2006. *Muslim teen Seek Belief in its Perfect Form.* Globe and Mail

Alain, M. 2001, The Trapeze Artists and the Ground Crew Police Cooperation and Intelligence Exchange Mechanisms in Europe and North America: a Comparative Empirical Study. *Policing and Society, 2001, Vol. 11*

Alberts, David S., John J. Garstka, Frederick P. Stein, 1999, *Network Centric Warfare: Developing and Leveraging Information Superiority.* Washington DC: C4ISR Cooperative Research Program

Aldrich, R.J. 2004 'Transatlantic Intelligence and Security Co-operation'. *International Affairs Journal, Vol. 80, No. 4*

Alvaro, Alexander, 14 April 2007, Developing Europol towards Efficiency and Accountability. Presentation during the Third Challenge Training School on Police and Judicial Cooperation in the Third Pillar of the European Union, Brussels

Amghar S.Boubekeur A and Emerson M. 2007, *European Islam: Challenges for society and public Policy,* Centre for European Policy Studies. Brussels

Andrew, Christopher and Mitrokhin, Vasili, 2005, The World Was Going Our Way: The KGB and the Battle for the Third World. New York: Basic Books

Andrew, Christopher and Oleg Gordievsky, 1990, *KGB, the Inside Story of its Foreign Operations from Lenin to Gorbachev,* London: Hodder & Stoughton

Argomaniz J, 2011. The EU and Counter-Terrorism: Politics, polity and policies after 9/11, London and New York: Routledge

Ascher K. 1987. *The Politics of Privatization*, Macmillan, London

Bamford James. 2002. *Body of Secrets. How America's NSA and Brittan's GCHQ Eavesdrop on the World*. Arrow Books, London

Barnad C. 2011. *Using procurement law to enforce labour standards*. Oxford University Press.

Beach, D. 2005, *The Dynamics Of European Integration: Why And When EU Institutions Matter*, Basingstoke, Palgrave Macmillan.

Bean, H. 2007, "The DNI's Open Source Centre: An Organizational Communication Perspective." *International Journal of Intelligence and Counterintelligence, Vol. 20, No. 2*, summer.

Beckman, James, 2007, *Comparative Legal Approaches to Homeland Security and Anti-Terrorism Homeland Security Series*, Ashgate.

Bennett Richard. 2002. *Espionage. Spies & Secrets*, Virgin Books, London

Bergeron, Kenneth D. 2002, *Tritium on Ice: The Dangerous New Alliance of Nuclear Weapons and Nuclear Power*. Cambridge, MIT Press.

Betts, Richard. *Enemies of Intelligence: Knowledge and Power in American National Security*, New York: Columbia University Press, 2007.

Bochel, H. Defty, A. and Kirkpatrick, J. 2014, *Watching the Watchers Parliament and the Intelligence Services. Basingstoke*: Palgrave Macmillan.

Bochel, H., Defty, A. and Dunn, A. 2010, *scrutinizing the secret state: parliamentary oversight of the intelligence and security agencies*. Policy & Politics

Brandon, James. August 2015, "Rise of Islamic State Reignites British Radicalization Threat." *Terrorism Monitor*.

Brewer John. D and Gareth. 1998. *Northern Ireland, 1921–1998*, Macmillan Press, London.

Bruce S. 1992. *The Red Hand: Protestant paramilitaries in Northern Ireland*, Oxford University Press.

Buckly A. and Kenny M.C. 1995, *Negotiating Identity: Rhetoric, Metaphor and social drama in Northern Ireland*, Smithsonian Institute Press

Budge, I., Crewe, I., McKay, D. and Newton, K. 2001, *The New British Politics*. Essex: Pearson,

Cabinet Office, 2010, *National Intelligence Machinery*.

Caldicott, Helen. 2002, *The New Nuclear Danger: George W. Bush's Military-Industrial Complex*. New York: The New Press

Castagna, Michael, 1997, "Virtual Intelligence: Reengineering Doctrine for the Information Age" *International Journal of Intelligence and Counterintelligence, 10, 2*

Chase, Alston, 2003. *Harvard and the Unabomber: The Education of an American Terrorist*. New York: W. W. Norton.

Chatham House Report, 2011, *Cyber Security and the UK's Critical National Infrastructure*

Chesterman, S. 2006, "Does the UN Have Intelligence?" *Survival, Vol. 48, No. 3, Autumn*, London.

Clarke, James W. 2012, *Defining Danger: American Assassins and the New Domestic Terrorists*. New Brunswick: Transaction Publishers

Coolsaet, R. 2010, "EU Counterterrorism strategy: Value-added or chimera?" *International Affairs, Vol. 86, No. 4*

Coolsaet, Rik. 2011, *Jihadi Terrorism and the Radicalization Challenge: European and American Experiences*. Farnham: Ashgate.

Coulter C. 1997, *Contemporary Northern Irish Society: An Introduction*, Pluto Press, London.

Crawford C. 2003, *Inside the UDA: Volunteers and Violence*, Pluto Press, London.

Davis, Jack. "Improving CIA Analytic Performance: DI Analytic Priorities." Sherman Kent Center for Intelligence Analysis, *Occasional Papers, v.l, no. 3.* Washington, DC: Central Intelligence Agency, September 2002.

Deucher, R. and Holligan C. 2010, *Gangs, Sectarianism and Social Capital: A Qualitative Study of Young People in Scotland.*

Dockrill, Michael L and David French. 1996, *Strategy and Intelligence: British Policy during the First World War*. Rio Grande, OH: Hambledon Press.

Duefer, Charles. 2009. "Hide and Seek: The Search for Truth in Iraq." *Public Affairs*, New York.

Engerman, David C. 2009. Jihadology: How the creation of Sovietology should guide the study of today's threats. *Foreign Affairs*, December 8. http://www.foreignaffairs.com/node/65670.

Ephron, Dan and Silvia Spring. 2008. "A gun in one hand, a pen in the other: The Army is spending millions to hire 'experts' to analyze Iraqi society. If only they could find some." *Newsweek*, April 12.

Ellison Graham, and Smyth Jim, 2000, *The Crowned Harp: Policing Northern Ireland*, Pluto Press, London

English, Richard, 2003, *Armed Struggle: A History of IRA*, MacMillan, London

Evan. G. and Duffy M. 1997, "Beyond the Sectarian Divide: The social Bases and Political consequences of Nationalist and Unionist Party Competition in Northern Ireland." *British Journal of Political Science*

Fair C. Christine. 2007. "Militant Recruitment in Pakistan: A New Look at the Militancy-Madrasa-Connection," *Asian Policy*.

Ferguson, Charles D, William C. Potter. 2004. *The Four Faces of Nuclear Terrorism*, Monterey Institute of International Studies.

Fingar, T. 2011, *Reducing Uncertainty: Intelligence Analysis And National Security*, Stanford, CA: Stanford University Press

Flakes, Elliott S, W.D, 1999, *Northern Ireland, A Political Dictionary, 1968–1999*, Belfast, Blackstaff Press

Friedrichs, J, 2008, *Fighting Terrorism And Drugs. Europe And International Police Cooperation*, London and New York: Routledge

Frost, Robin M. 2005. *Nuclear terrorism after 9/11, Abingdon*: Routledge for the International Institute for Strategic Studies.

Ganguli Sumit and Devin T. Hagerty. 2006. *Fearful Symmetry: India-Pakistan Crisis in the Shadow of Nuclear Weapons.* Seattle, W.A, University of Washington Press.

Ganguli Sumit and S. Paul Kapur. 2009. *Nuclear Proliferation in South Asia: Crisis Behaviour and the Bomb.* Routledge, New York.

Gavin, Francis J. 2012. *Nuclear statecraft: history and strategy in America's atomic age.* Cornell University Press

Gibson, David R. 2012. *Talk at the brink: deliberation and decision during the Cuban Missile Crisis.* Princeton: Princeton University Press.

Han, Henry Hyunwook. 1993. *Terrorism & Political Violence: Limits & Possibilities of Legal Control*, Oceana Publications, New York

Harvey, Frank P. 2008. *The Homeland Security Dilemma: Fear, Failure and the Future of American Insecurity.* Routledge, London.

Harvey, Frank P. 2008. *The Homeland Security Dilemma: Fear, Failure, and the Future of American Insecurity.* Contemporary Security Studies

Hay, Douglas and Francis G. Snyder, 1989, *Policing and Prosecution in Britain, 1750–1850*, Clarendon Press

Hillebrand, Claudia, 2012, *Counter-Terrorism Networks in the European Union: Maintaining Democratic Legitimacy after 9/11.* Oxford: Oxford University Press

Hoffman, Bruce; Reinares, Fernando. 2014, "The Evolution of the Global Terrorist Threat: From 9/11 to Osama bin Laden's Death." *Columbia Studies in Terrorism and Irregular Warfare*, New York, Columbia University Press

Howie, Luke. 2012. *Witnesses to terror: understanding the meanings and consequences of terrorism.* Basingstoke: Palgrave Macmillan

Howitt, Arnold M. 2003. *Countering terrorism: dimensions of preparedness.* Cambridge, Mass.: MIT Press.

Hughes, Frank J. and David Schum. *Evidence Marshalling and Argument Construction*, Washington, DC: Joint Military Intelligence College, Student Course Notes.

"Intelligence Organizations in Combating Armed Groups," *Journal of Public and International Affairs*, 2, Princeton: Princeton University Press, 200.

Isenberg, David. 2007. "Touchy, feely in the kill chain." *Asia Times Online*, Dec. 18.

Isenberg, David. 2009. "Dogs of War: The good, the bad and the contractor." *UPI.com*, March 27.

Jervis, Robert. "What's Wrong with the Intelligence Process?" *International Journal of Intelligence and Counterintelligence* 1, no. 2 spring 1986

Johnson, Douglas H. "2004–2010. Sources of Intelligence: A Bibliography of the Monthly Sudan Intelligence Report". Volume 11, Number 1, *Northeast African studies*

Johnson, Loch. "The Aspin-Brown Intelligence Inquiry: Behind the Closed Doors of a Blue Ribbon Commission," *Studies in Intelligence 48, no. 3 2004*

Johnson, Loch. 1989, *Seven Sins of Strategic Intelligence, in America's Secret Power: The CIA in a Democratic Society*, New York: Oxford University Press

Johnston, Les. 1999, *Policing in Britain, Longman Criminology Series*, Longman.

Kent, Sherman, 1966, *Strategic Intelligence for American World Policy*. Princeton, NJ: Princeton University Press.

Khan Saira. 2009. *Nuclear Weapons and Conflict Transformation, The Case of India-Pakistan*. Routledge Taylor and Francis Group, London

Klein, Gary. 2002, *Intuition at Work - Why Developing Your Gut Instinct Will Make You Better at What You Do*. New York: Doubleday

Krepton Michael. 2009. *Better Safe than Sorry: The Ironies of Living with the Bomb*. Stanford University Press, USA.

Krotz, Ulrich and Schild Joachim, 2013. *Shaping Europe: France, Germany, and Embedded Bilateralism from the Elysee Treaty to Twenty-First Century Politics*. Oxford University Press, UK.

Lan Bellany. 2007. *Terrorism and Weapons of Mass Destruction: Responding to the Challenge*. Routledge, London

Lawday, David. 2000, *Policing in France and Britain, Restoring confidence locally and nationally*, Franco–British Council. London.

Lewis, Jeffrey. 2014. *Paper Tiger: China's Nuclear Posture*. International Institute for Strategic Studies, London.

Lian, W. 2010. Talibanization in the Tribal Area of Pakistan, *Journal of Middle Eastern and Islamic Studies*.

Luongo, Kenneth N. and Naeem Salik, December, 1, 2007. "Building Confidence in Pakistan's Nuclear Security," *Arms Control Today*.

MacEachin, Douglas. CIA 1996, *Assessments of the Soviet Union: The Record versus the Charges*. Washington, DC: Central Intelligence Agency, Centre for the Study of Intelligence

Mawby, Rob and Dr Alan Wright, 2005, *Police Accountability in the United Kingdom*. Keele University, UK.

McCarthy, Mary. "The National Warning System: Striving for an Elusive Goal," *Defence Intelligence Journal 3, no. 1, spring 1994*

Messervy-Whiting, G. 2004, *Intelligence Cooperation in the European Union*, Centre for Studies in Security and Diplomacy, University of Birmingham.

Muller-Wille, Bjorn, "For your eyes only? Shaping an intelligence community within the EU," *Occasional Papers*, Institute for Security Studies, No.50, January 2004.

Nomikos, John M., 'The European Union's Proposed Intelligence Service', *PINR, June 2005*

Odom, William E. 2003, *Fixing Intelligence: for a More Secure America*. New Haven: Yale University Press

Omand, David. 2010. *Securing the State*. Hurst & Company London.

Pappas, Aris A. and James M. Simon, Jr. The Intelligence Community: 2001–2015, *Studies in Intelligence 46, no.1 2002*

Perrow, Charles. 1984, *Normal Accidents: Living with High-Risk Technologies*. New York: Basic Books

Ronczkowski, M.R. 2006, *Terrorism and Organized Hate Crime: Intelligence Gathering, Analysis, and Investigations*. CRC Press, Boca Raton: US

Raimondo, Justin. 2009. The Afghan 'Experiment': When all else fails, mobilize the social scientists! *AntiWar.com*, December 11.

Reid, Tim. 2009. Freedom for US contractor Don Ayala who shot dead handcuffed Taleban killer. *The Times*, May 9. http://www.timesonline.co.uk/tol/news/world/us_and_americas/article6251000.ece

Renzi, Fred, Lt. Col. 2006. Networds: Terra incognita and the case for ethnographic intelligence. *Military Review*, Sep-Oct.

Ricks, Thomas E. 2010. The Flynn Report (V): How to feed the beast. *Foreign Policy*, January 18.

Riechmann, Debb. 2009". NATO official: US intel lacking in Afghanistan." *Associated Press*, January 5.

Roberts, Audrey. 2009. A unique approach to peacekeeping: Afghanistan and the Human Terrain System. *Journal of International Peace Operations*, 5 (2) Sept-Oct

Schmid, A. P. 2011. *The Routledge handbook of terrorism research*, New York: Routledge.

Silke, A., ed. 2004. *Research on terrorism: Trends, achievements and failures*. London: Frank Cass.

Simon, Herbert. 1997, *Administrative Behavior*, New York: The Free Press

Smith, M. L. R. 1996, *Fighting for Ireland: The Military Strategy of the Irish Republican Movement*, London: Routledge

Smithson, Amy E. and Leslie-Anne Levy. "Ataxia: The Chemical and Biological Threat and the US Response." *Report no. 35, Henry L. Stimson Center, Oct 2000*

Stefik, Mark and Barbara Stefik, 2004, *Breakthrough: Stories and Strategies of Radical Innovation.* Cambridge, MA: MIT Press

Stern, Jessica. 1999, *The Ultimate Terrorists.* Cambridge: Harvard University Press

Stevenson, Jonathan. "Africa's Growing Strategic Resonance." *Survival, vol. 45, no. 4, Winter 2003-04*

Timmerman, Kenneth R. 2003, *Preachers of Hate: Islam and the War on America.* Random House, New York

Toolis, Kevin. 1996, *Rebel Hearts: Journeys Within the IRA's Soul.* St. Martin's Press

Travers, Russ. 1996, "The Coming Intelligence Failure," *Studies in Intelligence 40, no. 2*

Tucker, Jonathan B. 2000, *Toxic Terror: Assessing Terrorist Use of Chemical and Biological Weapons.* Cambridge: MIT Press

Tucker, Jonathan B. and Robert P. Kadlec, "Infectious Disease and National Security," *Strategic Review*, vol. 29, no. 2, Spring 2001.

United States Department of State Report, 23 May 2003, "Foreign Terrorist Organizations"

Van Bruinessen, Martin. "Genealogies of Islamic Radicalism in post-Suharto Indonesia," *South East Research*, vol. 10, no. 2, 2002.

Varshney, Ashutosh. 2002, *Competing National Imaginations, in Ethnic Conflict and Civic Life: Hindus and Muslims in India.* New Haven: Yale University Press

Volpi, Frederic, 2008. *Transnational Islam and Regional Security*, Routledge, London.

Walsh, Patrick F. 2011. *Intelligence and intelligence analysis.* Routledge, Taylor and Francis, London.

Weinberg, L. 2005. *Global terrorism: A beginner's guide.* Oxford: Oneworld

Wellock Thomas R. 1998. *Opposition to Nuclear Power in California, 1958–1978.* Madison, University of Wisconsin Press.

Wenger, Andreas and Wollenmann Reto. 2007. *Bioterrorism: Confronting a Complete Threat.* Lynne Rienner Publishers London

Whitaker, D. J. 2007. *Terrorism reader*, London, Routledge

White, J. R. 2013. *Terrorism and homeland security*, Belmont, CA: Wadsworth

Whitney, Craig R. 2005. "The WMD Mirage: Iraq's Decade of Deception and America's False Premises for War," *Journal of Public Affairs*, New York

Wilkinson, P. 2000. "The Strategic Implications of Terrorism," in: Sondhi, M.L. (ed.) *Terrorism and Political Violence. A Sourcebook*, Har-anand Publications, India

Yoshihara Toshi and James R. Holmes, 2012, *Strategy in the Second Nuclear Age: Power Ambitions and the Ultimate Weapon.* Georgetown University Washington DC.

Yusafzai Hamid Iqbal. 2011. *The US Factor in Pak-Afghan Relations Post 9/11.* Lambert Academic Publishing, Germany

Zaeef, Abdul Salam, *My Life with the Taliban*, London: Hurst and Company, 2009.

Zahab, Mariam Abu, and Olivier Roy, 2004, *Islamist Networks: The Afghan-Pakistan Connection*, London: C. Hurst

Printed in the United States
By Bookmasters